The Lost Sayings
of Jesus

Books in the
SkyLight Illuminations Series

The Lost Sayings of Jesus

Teachings from Ancient Christian,
Jewish, Gnostic, and Islamic Sources—
Annotated & Explained

Translation & Annotation
by Andrew Phillip Smith

Foreword by Stephan A. Hoeller

Walking Together, Finding the Way
SKYLIGHT PATHS®
PUBLISHING
Woodstock, Vermont

The Lost Sayings of Jesus:
Teachings from Ancient Christian, Jewish, Gnostic, and Islamic Sources—
Annotated & Explained

2006 First Printing
Translation, annotation, and introductory material © 2006 by Andrew Phillip Smith

For information regarding permission to reprint material from this book, please mail or
fax your request in writing to SkyLight Paths Publishing, Permissions Department, at
the address / fax number listed below, or e-mail your request to permissions@
skylightpaths.com.

Library of Congress Cataloging-in-Publication Data
The lost sayings of Jesus : teachings from ancient Christian, Jewish, Gnostic, and
Islamic sources, annotated & explained / translation and annotation by Andrew Phillip
Smith ; foreword by Stephan A. Hoeller.
p. cm. — (SkyLight illuminations)
Includes bibliographical references (p.   ).
ISBN-13: 978-1-59473-172-3
ISBN-10: 1-59473-172-1
1. Jesus Christ—Words. I. Smith, Andrew Phillip, 1966– II. Series.

BT306.L67 2006
229'.92—dc22

2005036647

10 9 8 7 6 5 4 3 2 1
Manufactured in the United States of America
Cover design: Walter C. Bumford III
Cover art: Jesus by Chris Sofopoulos © 2005 by Chris Sofopoulos (www.pbase.com/sofo)

SkyLight Paths Publishing is creating a place where people of different spiritual
traditions come together for challenge and inspiration, a place where we can
help each other understand the mystery that lies at the heart of our existence.

SkyLight Paths sees both believers and seekers as a community that increasingly transcends traditional boundaries of religion and denomination—people
wanting to learn from each other, *walking together, finding the way.*

SkyLight Paths, "Walking Together, Finding the Way" and colophon are trademarks of
LongHill Partners, Inc., registered in the U.S. Patent and Trademark Office.

Walking Together, Finding the Way
Published by SkyLight Paths Publishing
A Division of LongHill Partners, Inc.
Sunset Farm Offices, Route 4, P.O. Box 237
Woodstock, VT 05091
Tel: (802) 457-4000   Fax: (802) 457-4004
www.skylightpaths.com

For my wife and son

Contents ☐

Foreword ☐

Stephan A. Hoeller

The figure of the founder of the Christian religion has always presented a challenge to believers and nonbelievers alike. Referring to the earliest period of the history of Christendom, we find in the Gospel of Matthew (16.13) an account of Jesus questioning his disciples concerning their view of him. Their answers are largely reflective of the diverse opinions circulating at the time among the populace of Judea: "Some say that thou art John the Baptist, some Elias, and others Jeremias, or one of the prophets." It would seem that conditions bearing on this subject have not changed all that much since the times described by Matthew. There are a bewildering number of characterizations of Jesus today, most of which contradict each other markedly.

Those of us of an appropriate age may remember *Jesus Christ Superstar,* an entertaining and provocative play of the 1960s, where Jesus appears as a somewhat abrasive critic of society. A similar note was struck a few years later by the so-called liberation theologians, who saw Jesus as a revolutionary, pure and simple—a kind of first-century Che Guevara. Scholarly popularizers like Hugh J. Schonfield and John M. Allegro represented Jesus as either a scheming politician or a psychedelic-phallic messiah of dubious intentions. The list goes on and culminates in the excitement caused by several popular books published toward the end of the twentieth century (and in the early years of the twenty-first) which represent fantasies about Jesus married to Mary Magdalene as historical fact. Along radically different lines, we may note the revival of nineteenth-century intellectual excesses proclaiming that Jesus was a purely mythological figure compounded from diverse mythologems of previous times.

Jesus the revolutionary; the paterfamilias; the schemer; the mythic fiction—so many Jesuses and so much confusion!

The confusion surrounding the figure of Jesus stands a good chance of being reduced when the *logia* (sayings) attributed to Jesus are brought into public view. In addition to its many other merits, this potential of clarification is one of the great benefits bestowed on us by the comprehensive collection of sayings of Jesus, presented to us here by Andrew Phillip Smith. By availing yourself of this collection of sayings, you may arrive at certain, well-founded deductions regarding the teachings—as well as to some extent the character and mission—of Jesus. Certainly these sayings do *not* reveal a wild-eyed revolutionary, a conniving schemer, or even the likely progenitor of a secret royal bloodline. But so many sayings—many of which unquestionably reveal a common source—*do* indicate a historical personage of quite distinct character and orientation who stands behind this plethora of utterances. Those who want to receive authentic glimpses of Jesus may do so by consulting the sayings recorded and insightfully commented upon in this book.

"In the beginning was the Word." Thus begins the celebrated prologue to the Gospel of John. It is quite likely that the Christian religion also had its beginning with the words uttered by its founder, who in turn was often referred to by his mystical title, "the Logos." The available evidence indicates that the founder of the Christian religion practiced a twofold ministry. First, he functioned as a teacher who offered verbal exhortations of a special kind. As some sources, such as the Gospel of Thomas, indicate, his sayings were often designed to induce transformative changes in the consciousness of his listeners. (Sayings in the Gospel of Thomas have been likened to Zen koans.) The substance of most sayings addresses itself not so much to people's thinking minds, but rather to their incipient intuitive insight; the words intend not merely to inform but to stimulate latent insights and wisdom.

Second, Jesus was a hierophant who instituted mysteries into which he initiated those whom he deemed worthy. These initiatory procedures subsequently became known as sacraments in Western Christendom but are still called mysteries in the Orthodox Church. The Gospel of Philip, a Palestinian Gnostic treatise, lists five of these initiatory mysteries, although some scholars have discovered that the treatise actually mentions seven.

These considerations bring us to a most important issue. The discovery in 1945 of a large collection of Christian writings of Gnostic orientation has brought the subjects of Gnosticism and Gnostic scriptures into an entirely novel focus. It has become evident to many that the long-held notion of the existence of a mainstream, majority church in early Christendom is, in fact, incorrect. For about two centuries numerous Christianities existed side by side, one of them eventually becoming sufficiently established to declare the alternative schools heretical. Among these so-called heresies, the earliest and most important was what at a later time came to be referred to as Gnosticism. Gnostics were the followers of the first and in many ways most fascinating alternative Christianity; they were Christian mystics who held that salvation was achieved neither by faith nor by works, but rather by *gnosis,* the knowledge of the true realities of being. Gnostics employed both mysteries (sacraments) and insight-inducing sayings. They traced both of these modalities back to Jesus.

The four main categories of sayings listed in the present work (Christian, Jewish, Gnostic, and Islamic) all contain elements that have a relationship with Gnosticism, although only one may be unequivocally named. It is widely recognized, for instance, that the Apostolic Acts named for Peter, Andrew, Philip, John, and Thomas all contain numerous passages that are purely Gnostic. The reputed author of these acts was one Leucius Charinus, who was more than a little Gnostic—as indeed were many other early fathers of the church who preserved sayings of Jesus, among them Clement and Origen. The secret sayings of Jesus certainly represent a most important connection between Gnostic Christianity and Jesus himself.

In recent years a certain terminological ambivalence appears to have arisen regarding the term "Gnosticism." Some prominent writers have abandoned the use of this term and have adopted the substitute "alternative Christianity" instead. The fact remains that there existed a powerful tendency in the early Christian communities to embrace salvation through spiritual knowledge and other premises of what constitutes the Gnostic tradition.

Hans Jonas wrote that in order to understand Gnostic teachings, one needed something like a musical ear whereby to discern the subtleties of this worldview. Andrew Phillip Smith, in addition to his fine scholarship, possesses this musical ear. Since Gnosis runs through the numerous sayings like a golden thread, such an inner sensitivity is a most important ingredient of a work of this nature. The true source of such sayings is in a very real sense beyond the natural world and personal human psychology. Before, during, and after the time of Jesus and his apostles, human beings in states of exalted Gnosis have lifted their consciousness to transmundane heights of spiritual vision. It is thus that their utterances, their sayings, acquired the status of *logoi sophon,* true words of wisdom. In *Simon Magus,* G. R. S. Mead, an inspired early translator of such words, wrote, "The illumined soul that quits its prisonhouse, to bathe in the light of infinitude, can only recollect flashes of the Vision Glorious once it returns again to earth." The secret sayings here expertly translated and provided with brief, insightful commentaries, are in the nature of such "flashes of the Vision Glorious." May they illuminate the minds and hearts of many, as was the intention of those who wrote them down long ago for the spiritual benefit of humankind.

Introduction □

Jesus taught through the spoken word, using parables, proverbs, and pithy aphorisms. The gospels contained in the Christian New Testament are the best-known repository for the sayings of Jesus, and the parables, proverbs, and other sayings in these have made their way into the everyday life of many languages and cultures. The Sermon on the Mount, Matthew's artistic arrangement of some of Jesus's sayings, is considered to be one of the pinnacles of world religious literature. Parables such as the Good Samaritan and the Prodigal Son are part of the inheritance of humanity.

Although the canon of the New Testament is definitive for Christians, and the four gospels have pride of place within that canon, these writings were only a small part in the literature of early Christianity. Finds like the Gnostic library at Nag Hammadi in Egypt in 1945 (or, for Judaism, the Dead Sea Scrolls) have continued to provoke widespread interest since their discovery and subsequent publication. The discovery of the Gospel of Thomas, a collection of sayings of Jesus in Codex II of the Nag Hammadi library, which many scholars date to the first century, has emphasized the importance of the sayings of Jesus within the early tradition.[1]

The Gospel of Thomas has received widespread recognition, but many people are surprised to learn that an extensive body of Jesus's sayings are preserved in sources outside of the canonical gospels and the Gospel of Thomas. The Christian materials are found mainly in excerpts from the church fathers, in recently discovered fragments of lost gospels, and as additions to the canonical gospels in certain ancient manuscripts. Jewish Christians had their own gospels, and fragments of these have survived in quotation; a few references are made to Jesus in the Talmud and in later Jewish literature. Other Gnostic writings in the Nag Hammadi collection contain speech attributed to Jesus, chiefly in discussion with his disciples in dialogue form. An extensive body of tradition is also scattered throughout Islamic texts, in the Qur'an and in quotations by Sufi writers. Because these sayings have been collected piecemeal by scholars over the course of more than a century, they have never had the kind of media attention that has aided the recognition of finds such as the Nag Hammadi texts. Many of the sayings from these lesser-known sources are of equal value to those found in the canonical gospels or in Thomas, but they are even more striking because of their unfamiliarity. They typically emphasize the understanding of Jesus as a teacher, not as a miracle worker or messiah.

The Sayings Tradition

Throughout history spiritual teachers and religious leaders have found that they can crystallize their understandings in short, pithy sayings. Compilations such as the sayings of Buddha in the Dhammapada, the Tao te Ching of Lao Tzu, the Hadith of Muhammad, the aphorisms of Gurdjieff, the rabbinical Pirkei Avot, and the sayings of the Christian desert fathers come to mind. By the time of Jesus, the sayings collection was already an ancient genre, with examples in the Hebrew Bible and Apocrypha such as the Book of Proverbs and Ecclesiasticus, and from Egyptian literature, such as The Maxims of Ptahhotpe, The Teaching for Merikare, and The Instruction of Amenemope. The Hellenistic Greek culture that to various degrees influenced the Near East of that time offered examples such as Diogenes Laertius and, in the early second century, the Discourses of Epictetus.

A huge variety of material has contributed to the making of this book. The sources used range from the disapproving citations of the church fathers and quirky ancient editions of the New Testament to the exalted dialogues of the Gnostic redeemer Jesus and his disciples; to fragments of lost gospels found in Egyptian rubbish heaps and a cache of Gnostic texts hidden in a jar to obscure medieval homilies and the vast and rich literature of the Muslim world. Even the historically questionable results of spiritual "channeling" and the dubious productions of forgers and hoaxers contribute to the final section.

A saying of Jesus that is outside of the canonical gospels is called an agraphon (singular) or agrapha (plural). This Greek word means "an unwritten thing," and because the agrapha are not included in the four gospels, they are considered not to have been written down. This is obviously a rather contradictory term, since the only reason that we have the agrapha is because they were written down, albeit not in the four gospels. The term *agrapha* is still commonly used for these sayings, but extracanonical or noncanonical saying is a more accurate usage. A German scholar named Alfred Resch was the first to compile a thorough collection of the agrapha, first published in 1889, and he included 291 sayings, long before the Nag Hammadi library was discovered and before the Islamic sayings were properly collected. A succession of scholars continued to add material and to refine the work begun by Resch. Some of Resch's sayings, on close inspection, were not really assigned to Jesus, and a number of quotations that begin "the Lord said" were actually quotations from the Hebrew Bible or Jewish pseudepigrapha, the noncanonical Jewish texts, and not intended to be taken as sayings of Jesus. The best modern scholarly collection is William Stroker's *Extracanonical Sayings of Jesus*, though it concentrates on the Christian material at the expense of Gnostic material, and ignores the Islamic agrapha altogether. Other modern collections include William G. Morrice's *The Hidden Sayings of Jesus* and Marvin Meyer's *The Unknown Sayings of Jesus*.

The vast Arabic and Persian literature of Islam has turned out to be a rich source of agrapha. Many profound and beautiful texts are still little-known in the West, despite the extraordinary surge of interest in the poets Rumi and Hafiz, and an even larger number of texts have never even been translated into European languages. D. S. Margoliouth, professor of Arabic at Oxford, was the first to collect these, mainly utilizing the sayings found in *Revival of the Religious Science,* an extensive work written by al-Ghazali, the brilliant eleventh- and twelfth-century Sufi philosopher. Spanish scholar Michael Asin translated 233 of these Muslim sayings into Latin, and James Robson's *Christ in Islam* remains a useful collection of both Qur'anic and Sufi material. Tarif Khalidi's recent *The Muslim Jesus* is the most extensive collection of them so far in English, but it excludes the Qur'anic material. Although the Muslim writers necessarily quote these sayings much later than their Christian and Jewish counterparts did, they may have inherited many of them from existing Christian traditions, so they should not be dismissed out of hand as medieval inventions.

No single collection of the words of Jesus will ever contain everything attributed to him. For academics, the collection and assessment of Islamic material will always be regarded as a separate endeavor because of the entirely different time period and languages. For the general reader, a complete collection would contain too many redundancies and too much repetition for it to be of interest.[2] Even so, the present book represents the fullest single collection available for the general reader.

The Question of Authenticity

All of the sayings in this collection are attributed to someone called Jesus, often referred to by titles such as "the Lord" or "the Savior." But were they really spoken by the historical Jesus? The issue of the authenticity of the sayings is a complex one, and the question of which sayings go back to a historical first-century Galilean Jew named Yeshu or Yeshua in Aramaic, Iesous in Greek, Isa in the Islamic tradition, and Jesus in English, is not fundamental to the present book. Nevertheless, the issue of authenticity has to be addressed, and by the end of this discussion I hope that the reader will have a different view of the problem.

Jesus said things—unless one is willing to posit that there was no historical Jesus, that there was never a man called Jesus who is at the foundation of Christianity and bears some resemblance to the gospel accounts—of this we can be sure. The canonical gospels depict him as teaching his disciples individually and also teaching large groups of people—according to Mark, there is some difference between the specific teaching and the general teaching, whether in the material or just in the interpretation of the material. The things that he said were remembered by his companions and followers, passed on by word of mouth, eventually written down in lists, incorporated into accounts of his life, or referred to in letters, and then copied from manuscript to manuscript, whether the scribe was simply duplicating a text or incorporating it into a new work.

Jesus died in the 30s of the first century, and the earliest literary usage of the sayings material occurs in the four gospels and the Gospel of Thomas, written roughly from 70 C.E. onward. Thus, there is more than an entire generation between the lifetime of Jesus and the first extensive literary quotation of the sayings of Jesus. (The apostle Paul does refer to commandments of the Lord, and a few pieces in Paul's letters bear something of a resemblance to sayings of Jesus but are not quoted as such. Generally, Paul is not considered a reliable witness to the sayings tradition.)

Some sayings may have been spoken by Jesus only once; other sayings he might have repeated throughout his life. Not everything he said was original—he quoted from the Hebrew Bible and used proverbs that were part of the vast traditions of the Middle East and the Hellenistic civilization. Some (perhaps most) of what he said has strong parallels in other religious and philosophical teachings of the time, as for example the rabbinical teachers, the mystery religions, and the Greek Cynic philosophers.[3] But if a saying attributed to Jesus has a close parallel in another source, we find ourselves asking the question: Did Jesus actually say this, or is this something that originally belonged to another tradition and then, as Christianity gained momentum and spread into different countries, became absorbed into the tradition of Jesus sayings? Other sayings might have been put into the mouth of Jesus by the members of the early church, eager to have authoritative backing for their doctrines. How do we distinguish between the authentic and the inauthentic sayings of Jesus?

The sayings of Jesus are like a river flowing down from its mountain source. As the river gathers momentum, tributaries join it and become part of the river, swelling its flow. Before the river reaches the ocean and pours into it, it becomes a delta of small rivers and streams, joining and separating in a maze of little watercourses, confused and multitudinous, but all existing because of the course of the great river. When we investigate the sayings of Jesus, we have access only to the ocean and the delta. Once we get to the ocean, everything is from Jesus and we have no way of differentiating the source from the tributaries. Our best bet is to examine the myriad small streams, hoping that they will somehow tell us more about the rivers that fed them and the ultimate source.

For a long time, the question of authenticity seemed easy to answer: the genuine sayings of Jesus are those contained in the New Testament gospels. The mere fact that a gospel is contained within the canon of the Christian New Testament is still enough to guarantee the historical accuracy of its contents for many people, including the many scholars who are Christian apologists. From such a point of view, anything outside of the canonical gospels that sounds like the sayings within the gospels *may* be authentic, but this is unlikely, and the chances of finding a genuine saying of Jesus outside of the New Testament are slim. This approach is now known as canonical bias, and it is an uncritical and faith-based position.

Over the past couple of centuries, scholars have investigated the New Testament using the critical methods that have been developed. Quite a few of their discoveries can be easily verified by attentive reading of the gospels. Many people have noticed that the way Jesus speaks in the Gospel of John is different from the way he speaks in the other three gospels. In John, Jesus's speech consists mainly of long discourses. Jesus makes strong and extravagant claims as to his importance, particularly in the "I am" sections that are so prominent in the Fourth Gospel. In Matthew, Mark, and Luke, Jesus does not usually speak in this way, but rather more typically in pithy sayings and parables. The form of Jesus's speech in the Gospel of John is more developed and literary and so is further from oral tradition, and the possibility of it being directly derived from memories of Jesus's lifetime is significantly less.[4] So scholars naturally look to the other three gospels as a more reliable source of information on Jesus's speech and life.

If we place Matthew, Mark, and Luke in columns next to each other, we see that they share an overwhelming amount of material, including some verbatim and near-verbatim matches, much of which occurs in the same order in two or sometimes three of the gospels. Clearly, Matthew, Mark, and Luke have a relationship to each other that goes beyond the naive possibility that three different people wrote three independent accounts of Jesus's life. Neither is it likely that a continuous narrative—the form the Synoptic Gospels take—existed in oral tradition. The relationship among them is a literary relationship, which is the result of at least two of the gospels using another gospel as their source. The issue of which gospel depends on which is known in scholarship as the Synoptic problem, and the generally accepted solution to this is called the Two Source hypothesis, which argues that Mark was written first and was used as a basis for Matthew and Luke. These last two, in turn, also used a now-lost source named Q (from the German word *Quelle*, "source").[5] This means that Matthew and Luke did not necessarily know many of the sayings themselves, but took most of them from either from the Gospel of Mark or Q.

Investigating further, there are other reasons to doubt the authenticity of Jesus's sayings in the four gospels. Unless we wish (on unhistorical grounds) to give credence to all of the stories in the gospels as eyewitness accounts, we must assume that some of Jesus's words in the stories have been made up for the convenience of the narrative. Next, we find parallels to many of the sayings of Jesus in the Hellenistic and Jewish cultures of the first century and adjacent periods. As the snowball of the sayings tradition rolled down the hill, it grew, absorbing into it proverbs and sayings from other traditions.

Once we have admitted that not everything in the gospels attributed to Jesus was actually spoken by him, it is tempting to want to assess the genuineness of each saying and to form a core of historically reliable sayings of Jesus. The results that one obtains in determining which sayings are genuine seems to be very dependent on the degree of skepticism or credulity that one brings to the task. The process is essentially a negative one of whittling away at the inventory of sayings until one is happy with the results. How much whittling away one does depends on how rigorous one's conditions of authenticity or historicity are.[6]

Recent Scholarship

Scholars have tried hard to come up with criteria that might help us determine whether a saying is authentic. If a saying occurs independently in several sources, this is known as multiple attestation. The idea behind this is that if a number of people have written down a particular saying, and they haven't taken it from other writers, then it is likely to come from oral tradition, and hence be closer to the words of Jesus. Dissimilarity is another criterion: if a saying of Jesus would seem to be at odds with the religious background of his time, and the saying is known to be early, then it may be more likely that the saying contains material that is distinctive to Jesus. Coherence is yet another criterion by which a saying is considered more authentic: If it fits in with other sayings of Jesus, it makes a coherent whole with other sayings. If a saying provides difficulty for the gospel writers or other writers quoting it, then it is likely that the saying wasn't invented by the writer quoting it. All of these criteria have their own problems, but they allow us to examine aspects of the material in a useful way.

Some recent attempts to identify the genuine sayings of Jesus have included putting the noncanonical sayings, at least initially, on an even footing with the canonical material. In 1985, scholar Robert Funk opened the first meeting of a project titled the Jesus Seminar. The Jesus Seminar involved a huge number of North American scholars who voted on the authenticity of the sayings of Jesus. According to the Jesus Seminar, only 18 percent of the words attributed to Jesus in all Christian texts from the first three centuries (thus including many of the sayings given in this book) were actually spoken by him.

The influential John Dominic Crossan (incidentally, a member of the Jesus Seminar) separated traditions into different strata in an almost archaeological way. He included all of the noncanonical material and hypothetical sources such as the sayings material in Q and the collections of signs and miracles that scholars have postulated might underlie the Gospels of John and Mark. He ordered them chronologically and then looked at how many times a saying was quoted independently, classifying the material by its age and the number of times it was independently quoted. Thus, a saying from the earliest stratum that appeared independently three times would have a much greater weighting and therefore a greater claim to authenticity than a late saying that occurred only once. In a later book, *The Birth of Christianity*, Crossan proposed that the material common to the earliest layers of both Q and Thomas would necessarily precede either (assuming the independence of Thomas and the existence of Q).

While the results of research into the genuine sayings contained in the four gospels are ambiguous at best, many scholars have been hard-pressed even to take the agrapha, the sayings outside of the four gospels, seriously. A little more than a dozen agrapha have been generally considered for inclusion in the list of authentic sayings of Jesus. It is only recent attempts, like Crossan's or the Jesus Seminar, that have at the outset placed the noncanonical texts on an even footing with the four gospels.

The possibility of discovering the authentic sayings of Jesus is an exciting one, and the methods described above, if not the conclusions derived from those methods, are an attempt to be fair to all sayings of Jesus, whether in or out of the New Testament. But the result of such research is often a minimal Jesus.

If the results of scholarship could be considered definitive, then we could simply assign a core of sayings to Jesus and recognize that the surrounding material is, to extend the metaphor of fruit, the flesh and rind produced by early Christian writers. But none of the positive scholarly judgments can be considered definitive. The problem is that none of the early texts, or even the postulated sources of the texts, can definitely be shown to go back to Jesus. Even when Q is reconstructed by taking the material common to Matthew and Luke, but not to Mark, and highly sophisticated methods and analysis are used to re-create it to isolate and remove the factors that are most likely to belong to the editorial hands of Matthew and Luke, the resulting document displays its own concerns, and those concerns cannot necessarily be shown to be those of Jesus. Subsequent literary analysis of Q and stratification of it into different layers, the earliest layer consisting generally of wisdom teaching, runs into the same problem. The apostle Paul, author of the earliest Christian texts, is of little help, because the few quotes of his that have a tenuous connection to the gospel sayings are often quoted without reference to Jesus. So, if we apply truly rigorous historical standards, we have no sayings that can be reliably attributed to Jesus. The brilliance of methodology and the variety of approaches to the problem ultimately tell us that the evidence that we possess simply doesn't allow us to say for certain whether any saying of Jesus really goes back to him.

The Value of the Sayings

Now, while there is a core of scholars for whom the historical investigation of Jesus is only and uniquely a matter of intellectual curiosity, most of us are interested in Jesus because of our established religious backgrounds or because we are seeking spiritual meaning. Anyone who loves the sayings of Jesus will surely consider the parables of the Good Samaritan and the Prodigal Son to be among the finest of his parables, and the Sermon on the Mount to be his finest extended teaching. Yet the two parables occur only in Luke, and they have a number of characteristics that are typical of Luke's editorial (or redactional) hand. Do we lose anything if we decide that they were never spoken by Jesus? After all, the parable of the Prodigal Son is beautiful and profound whether it was spoken by Jesus or written by the author of the Gospel of Luke. Consider the following saying:

"Jesus said, 'It is better to serve others than to make others serve you.'" It sounds quite Yeshuine, and would fit well as one of the more authentic sayings in the present book. But it is, in fact, taken from the Sentences of Sextus, one of the texts found at Nag Hammadi, and no one has ever suggested that it is a saying of Jesus.

The various groups of people who preserved, added to, and recorded the teachings of Jesus—the Christian, Jewish, Gnostic, and Islamic writers referred to in this book—were not interested in Jesus for reasons of critical scholarship. Nor were they interested in compiling lists of sayings in an entirely neutral fashion. Yet the sayings and stories about Jesus, and the notions of his divine and human roles, defined Jesus for the people who used the great variety of texts that appear in this book.

I expect the reader to be able to switch hats at will while reading the sayings in this book. On the one hand, a saying of Jesus is just a saying attributed to Jesus—and that's it. Everything attributed to Jesus in this book and in the New Testament, and anywhere else, is a saying of Jesus. On the other hand (or wearing the other hat), I will occasionally discuss the authenticity of a particular saying. Some sayings are clearly nearer the fire, while others are far from the kingdom, to quote Gospel of Thomas saying 82. The good news for those who are at least as interested in spiritual teachings as they are in history is that a saying does not have to be historically Yeshuine to be spiritually useful.

What is certain is that the sayings in this book have defined Jesus for a great variety of religious and spiritual groups as much as the sayings in the canonical gospels have. Not only do these extracanonical sayings give us a chance of getting closer to the historical Jesus, but they also allow us to access the views of Jesus held by an incredible variety of cultures. The Jesus of Gnostics or Sufis or Jewish Christians is as worthy a figure, and as profound a teacher, as the Jesus of Catholic or Protestant Christianity.

A Note on the Translation ☐

Where the original text is in Greek or Coptic in Stroker's edition, that has been my source for translation. Where the texts are fragmentary (as is often the case with the Nag Hammadi material), I have generally avoided controversial reconstruction and have simply indicated lacunae by ellipses [...]. Where passages are reconstructed, I am dependent on the translations in James Robinson's edition, Bentley Layton's *The Gnostic Scriptures,* Robert J. Miller's *The Complete Gospels,* and Schneemelcher's *New Testament Apocrypha.* Selections in languages other than Greek or Coptic, and some of the Nag Hammadi material, are paraphrased using as many different translations as I had access to. The al-Ghazali material is paraphrased from Margoliouth, with reference to Robson and other translations, and the rest of the Islamic material is from Robson.

I acknowledge the generations of scholars who have collected the material, produced critical editions, and translated.

The sayings material in the Further Traditions section is, apart from the Manichaean and Mandaean material, taken directly from the English originals. The two short excerpts from the Jesus Sutras are taken from Martin Palmer's translation.

Where a saying is reported by another writer, as is often the case with material taken from the church fathers or from Islamic sources, I have generally removed the writer's own interjections.

In this book, the accurate and unprejudiced term *Hebrew Bible* will be used instead of the Christian term *Old Testament.* Since no accurate alternative exists for the term *New Testament,* I refer to the collection by its traditional Christian name.

Christian
Sayings

☐ Introduction to the Christian Sayings

In its early centuries, Christianity was full of diverse groups and points of view. When Constantine and Theodosian made Christianity into the state religion of the Roman Empire in the fourth century C.E., the march toward a consistent doctrine and universal church was under way, but a good deal of diversity survived for centuries afterward. The second and third centuries C.E. saw an explosion of creativity in Christianity; scholar Charles W. Hedrick recently counted thirty-four gospels, Christian and Gnostic, for which we have evidence. In the early second century, Papias reportedly collected five volumes of the sayings of Jesus, titled The Exposition of the Oracles of the Lord, which are now, unfortunately, lost.

Otherwise unknown sayings of Jesus and variations on the canonical sayings are scattered throughout early Christian writings. Quotations from the Gospel of the Egyptians, a lost gospel cited by Clement of Alexandria and Origen, among others, have fascinated scholars for decades. Scholarly church fathers such as Clement and Origen were usually careful to quote their sources, but many of the noncanonical sayings of Jesus are quoted in the course of sermons about legendary lives of the apostles without comment. The little-known Syrian tradition is particularly fruitful, its literary products stretching from Thomasine literature and the Diatessaron harmony, which produced a coherent narrative from the four canonical gospels, to later texts such as the Liber Graduum. Syria was also strongly connected with Gnosticism and with Mani, the founder of Manichaeanism.

Even centuries after Western Christianity had developed into orthodoxy, unusual sayings survived in a handful of medieval texts, and long-ignored ancient writings lingered in monastic libraries, such as the first-century Didache, found in the nineteenth century in a small monastery in Istanbul. Writings were lost not only through active heresy hunting but also as an indirect result of the new orthodoxy and the standardization of the canon. Christians lost their interest in noncanonical texts, and, because manuscript copying was an expensive and time-consuming process, much of the older apocryphal material was gradually allowed to rot away.

The Jesus that we find in these Christian extracanonical sayings is akin to the Jesus of the New Testament: he is a twin to the canonical Jesus, the outline of his features broadly similar, but the details differing. This Jesus speaks more in proverbs than in parables, and can be as terse and startling as the Jesus of the Gospel of Thomas or the Synoptics. There are plenty of hard sayings—statements that cause one to pause and wonder whether one is living one's life in the right way—but there is also much love.

1 Tucked away at the end of a long speech given by Paul to church members from Ephesus, these are said by Paul to be the words of "the Lord Jesus." Whether Jesus said it or not (and Paul is not known for accurate quotation of Jesus sayings, nor the author of Acts for historical veracity), a very similar version of this occurs as a Hellenistic proverb.

✦ The first letter of Clement is dated to the end of the first century, and is attributed to Clement of Rome, who in later tradition was bishop of Rome.

✦ The Apocryphal Acts of the Apostles are generally late second- and early third-century productions. They largely fit into the genre of ancient romance, with dangerous travels to foreign countries and shipwrecks looming large in these fictional narratives. Jesus sometimes gives a postresurrection appearance, and is sometimes quoted within the texts.

2 The inability of the disciples to understand Jesus while he was alive is a strong theme in the Gospel of Mark.

3 Peter's words in Latin, "Quo vadis?" have made this the most famous episode in the Apocrypha, and the surrounding story was made into an epic Hollywood film in 1951.

□ Christian Sayings

It is more blessed to give than to receive.[1]

—ACTS OF THE APOSTLES 20.35

Be merciful, so that you might obtain mercy; forgive, so that you may be forgiven. As you do, so will it be done to you. As you give, so will it be given to you. As you judge, so will you be judged. As you do good, so will goodness be done to you. The measure you measure out will be measured back to you.

—1 CLEMENT 13.1–2

Those who are with me have not understood me.[2]

—ACTS OF PETER 10

And when he saw him, he said: "Lord, where are you going?" And the Lord said to him: "I am going to Rome to be crucified." And Peter said to him: "Lord, are you being crucified again?" He said to him: "Yes, Peter, I am being crucified again."[3]

—ACTS OF PETER 35

4 Marriage imagery is commonly attributed to Jesus, hence much of the speculation about Jesus's marital status and his relationship to Mary Magdalene. It is very common in the Gospel of Philip, which shares some traditions with the Acts of Philip. But here it is just one among many beautiful metaphors.

5 This is the sort of pithy, thought-provoking saying that many see as being typical of Jesus. Despite its limited attestation, I would rate its likely authenticity high among noncanonical sayings.

6 Ransoming souls from idols refers to the Christian perception of pagans worshiping idols—false gods.

7 Jesus more or less has to guide Pilate through the motions of condemning him to death. A surprising number of apocryphal texts center around Pilate, including gospel-like literature and forged correspondences between Pilate and Tiberius, and Pilate and Herod. These legendary accounts are sympathetic to Pilate, to the extent that he became a saint in the Ethiopian church, having reputedly converted to Christianity after the death of Jesus.

Look, my bridal chamber is ready, but blessed is the one who is found within wearing his bright garment, for he receives the crown on his head. Look, the meal is ready, and blessed is he who is invited and is ready to go to the one who invited him. The field's harvest is great and the good laborer is blessed. See the lilies and all of the other flowers, and the good farmer is whoever first receives a part of them.[4]

—Acts of Philip 135

You must enter the kingdom of heaven through much tribulation.[5]

—*Prochorus*, Acts of John

Whoever ransoms souls from idols will be great in my kingdom.[6]

—Acts of Thomas 6

And he called Jesus and said to him, "What should I do with you?"

Jesus said to Pilate, "Do as it was given to you."

Pilate replied, "How was it given?"

Jesus said, "Moses and the prophets prophesied my death and resurrection."[7]

—Acts of Pilate 4.3

8   Although this dialogue is certainly historically dubious, it is a fascinating development of the tradition of Jesus's trial before Pilate. Far from maintaining silence, as he does in Mark, Matthew, and Luke, Jesus has plenty of profound comments to make. Some of the dialogue is common to the Gospel of John, but in John, Pilate has the last word. "'What is truth?' said jesting Pilate; and would not stay for an answer" as the English essayist Francis Bacon famously put it. Jesus not only gives an answer in the Acts of Pilate, he gives a profound one.

Pilate called for Jesus and said to him, "What are you accused of ... ? Don't you have anything to say?" Jesus answered him, "If my accusers were powerless, they, too, would say nothing. But each person has power—the power over his own mouth to speak good or evil. So they will use their power and see to it."

Later, Pilate once again entered the praetorium and took Jesus aside and asked him, "Are you the King of the Jews?" Jesus answered him, "Do you ask me on your own or did others tell you this about me?"

Pilate replied, "Am I a Jew? Your own nation and its chief priests have handed you over to me. Now tell me, what have you done?" Jesus told him, "My kingship is not of this world; else my followers would have fought against the Jews at my arrest. My kingship is not here and is not now."

Pilate said, "So you are a king, then!" Jesus answered, "You say that I am a king. I am. I was born and have come here so that everyone who is of the truth might hear my voice."

Pilate said to him, "What is truth?" Jesus answered, "Truth comes from heaven."

Pilate said, "Is there no truth on earth?" Jesus replied, "Yes, but you can easily see how those who speak the truth are judged by those in authority on earth."[8]

—ACTS OF PILATE 3.2–3

9 The Greek word *parousia* means "presence" and particularly had the meaning of the presence of a visiting king. As Christianity developed, it came to refer to the future second coming of Christ.

10 This saying also crops up in the Liber Graduum (see below). Both this and the Aphrahat text are Syrian documents, so this saying was clearly in circulation in Syria.

✦ Aphrahat was a fourth-century Syrian Christian writer.

11 Simon Peters's lack of faith in walking on the water is used as a metaphor for sinking down into the world—presumably losing oneself in the things that belong to the outer world.

12 In John 8.44, "You are from your father the Devil, and you choose to do your father's desires" is addressed to the Jews who dispute with Jesus in the Temple treasury. In John 8.36, the same Jews had referred to themselves as children of Abraham. This is most likely a variant of this, summed up as a saying.

13 In isolation, this saying is fairly unexceptionable. But the context is a discussion of the role of women in the eucharistic service: "John said, 'Have you forgotten, brothers, that our Master, when He had asked for the bread and wine, blessed them and said, "This is My body and My blood"? He did not allow the women to be with us.' Martha said; 'It is because of Mary, because he saw her laugh.' Mary said: 'That was not the reason why I laughed. He said to us before, when he taught that through the strong, the weak shall be saved.'"

✦ The Apostolic Church Ordinances is a third-century text that draws on earlier sources. It is primarily concerned with community rules and church law.

14 Acts 20.35: "In all this I have given you an example that by such work we must support the weak, remembering the words of the Lord Jesus, for he himself said, 'It is more blessed to give than to receive.'"

Whoever leaves everything through my name will receive eternal life at the Parousia.[9]

—AGATHANGELUS 65

Pray and do not tire.[10]

—*APHRAHAT*, DEMONSTRATION 4.16

Do not doubt, in case you sink down into the world, as Simon when he doubted began to sink down into the sea.[11]

—*APHRAHAT*, DEMONSTRATION 1.17

You are not the children of Abraham, but the children of Cain.[12]

—*APHRAHAT*, DEMONSTRATION 16.8

Through the strong, the weak shall be saved.[13]

—APOSTOLIC CHURCH ORDINANCES 2.6

The giver is more blessed than the receiver.[14]

—APOSTOLIC CONSTITUTIONS 4.2–3

✦ The Apostolic Constitutions is a fourth-century work written in the name of the first-century Clement of Rome.

15 The first-century text known as the Didache is quite concerned with the behavior of wandering Christian prophets who relied on the good-will of the local Christian communities to support them. Paul argues that he supports himself when he needs to. Evidently this, or some analog of it, was still a problem in the fourth century.

16 "Son of man" was used in Aramaic as a roundabout way of referring to oneself, and it seems to be in this sense that Jesus is using the phrase, not as a specific title for himself. This saying is sometimes assigned to the lost work The Traditions of Matthias.

✦ Clement of Alexandria was one of the most brilliant of the church fathers. He lived in the second and early third centuries and was head of the catechetical school at Alexandria. His works include the voluminous Stromata ("Miscellanies") from which many of these quoted sayings of Jesus are taken. Also see the sections on the Gospel of the Egyptians and the Jewish-Christian Gospel of the Hebrews.

17 A fairly definite example of a piece from Paul becoming part of the Jesus sayings tradition. See 1 Corinthians 7.10–11.

18 Family relationships are the source of much imagery in early Christianity. Jesus is depicted particularly in the Gospel of Mark as having a difficult relationship with his mother and brothers. Christians were a surrogate family to one another.

Woe to those who already have and receive more hypocritically, or who are able to maintain themselves yet want to receive from others. For each will give account to the Lord God on judgment day.[15]

—APOSTOLIC CONSTITUTIONS 4.2–3

When Zacchaeus, a head tax collector (though some say Matthias) heard that the Lord had seen fit to come to him, said, "Lord, I have given half my possessions as alms and if I have taken anything from someone by extortion, I will pay it back quadrupled."
Then the Lord said, "The son of man came today and found that which was lost."[16]

—CLEMENT OF ALEXANDRIA, STROMATA 4.6.35

Whoever is married should not send away his wife, and whoever is not married should not marry; whoever has determined not to marry because of abstinence should remain unmarried.[17]

—CLEMENT OF ALEXANDRIA, STROMATA 3.15.9

For my brothers and fellow heirs are those who do my Father's will. Therefore, do not say, "your father on earth," for there are masters on earth, but the Father is in heaven; from him comes every family in both heaven and earth.[18]

—CLEMENT, ECLOGUE PROPHETICAE 20

For my brothers and fellow heirs are those who do the will of my Father.

—CLEMENT, ECLOGUE PROPHETICAE 20.3

19 The female in this sense perhaps refers allegorically to the passions.

20 A very simple saying, but touching. Clement tells us that this was uttered as Jesus was "about to be offered up and to give himself as a ransom." So perhaps in the unknown source in which the saying was found by Clement the saying was uttered in the setting of the Last Supper or in the Garden of Gethsemane.

21 A variation on this: "My mystery is for me and those who are mine."

22 In an extended discussion of the beatitudes, Clement gives these as the opinion of "those who transpose the gospels." That is, he feels that these are just reworkings of existing material. They may come from lost gospels or traditions.

I have come to destroy the works of the female.[19]

—Gospel of the Egyptians, *Clement of Alexandria,*
Stromata 3.9.63

I give my love to you.[20]

—*Clement*, Quis Dives Salvetur 37.4 (Who Is the Rich Man
Who Shall Be Saved?)

My mystery is for me and for the children of my
house.[21]

—*Clement of Alexandria*, Stromata 5.10.63

Blessed are those who are persecuted for my sake, for
they will have a place where they will not be
persecuted.[22]

—*Clement of Alexandria*, Stromata 4.6.41

Blessed are they who are persecuted by righteousness,
for they shall be perfect.

—*Clement of Alexandria*, Stromata 4.6.41

Blessed are you when men shall hate you, when they
shall separate you, when they shall cast out your name
as evil, for the Son of Man's sake.

—*Clement of Alexandria*, Stromata 4.6.41

23 Codex Bezae is one of the earliest manuscripts of the New Testament. It contains many small variations when compared to other manuscript traditions. In two places it also contains additions to verses in the Gospel of Luke.

✦ Ancient manuscripts were copied by hand and no two copies of the New Testament before the invention of printing are absolutely identical in wording. While each manuscript has very tiny differences to its parent manuscript, the one from which it was copied, some manuscripts contain small amounts of extra material brought in from other, unknown sources. The story of the woman caught in adultery is a classic example. Although this story is very well known and is usually included after John 7.52, it does not belong there and appears in different places, including sometimes in Luke, in different manuscript copies. These additional sayings and stories are sometimes known as orphan stories and sayings.

24 Rabbinical law allowed all sorts of exceptions to working on the Sabbath, and Jesus himself is depicted as breaking Sabbath law. This saying, with its setting—which is as likely or unlikely to refer to an actual event as anything in the canonical gospels—indicates that it is whether one works knowingly that makes the difference.

25 The so-called Freer logion, from a fourth- or fifth-century manuscript now in the Freer Museum at the Smithsonian Institution, gives a different ending to the Gospel of Mark. It is clearly a late addition, but it caused quite some excitement back in the early twentieth century when the manuscript was discovered.

I have not come among you as one who dines, but as one who serves, and you have grown in my service as one who serves.²³

—CODEX BEZAE ADDITION TO LUKE 22.27–28

That same day, he saw a man working on the Sabbath, and he said to him, "Man, if you know what you do, you are blessed. But if you do not know, you are even more accursed and a lawbreaker."²⁴

—CODEX BEZAE ADDITION TO LUKE 6.4

The limit of the years of Satan is fulfilled: but other fearful things draw near. I was delivered to death by sinners so that they might return to the truth and sin no more, that they might inherit the spiritual and incorruptible glory of righteousness which is in heaven.²⁵

—FREER MS ADDITION TO MARK 16.14–15

Whoever is not like me is not like him who sent me. And whoever believes in me does not believe in me, but in him who sent me.

—FREER MS VARIANT (SYRIAC) TO JOHN 12.44

You do not know which spirit you belong to, for the Son of Man did not come to destroy people's lives but to save them.

—FREER MS VARIANT TO LUKE 9.55

26 Trying to thread a rope through a needle makes more immediate sense than trying to thread a camel through one. The Greek word *kamilos*, meaning "rope," is very similar to *kamêlos*, meaning "camel," and the Aramaic word *gamla*, can have both meanings. But rabbinic writings include a similar saying where it is easier for an elephant to go through a needle's eye, which was proverbially small, so it is more likely that "rope" is a later misinterpretation.

27 Widely attested in, for instance, Cyprian, Augustine, Hilary, Chromatus, and as a variant reading in the Irish Book of Armagh, this variation of the famous clause in the Lord's Prayer offers a subtly different view as to what is in our control.

✦ Cyprian was a third-century bishop of Carthage in North Africa.

28 The Dialogue between Christ and the Devil is a late and obscure Slavic text, but the images are vivid and distinctive.

29 Another example of a Pauline verse that is known to at least one writer as a saying of Jesus. Paul quotes this (or originates it) in Ephesians 4.26. The Dialogue of Adamantius is a fourth-century anti-heretical writing, composed of a discussion between the orthodox Adamantius and several varieties of Gnostics.

30 As a piece of advice, this is startling common sense. How can people have enemies if they love even those who hate them?

✦ The Didache, or the Teaching of the Twelve Apostles, was written in the late first century or early second century. It is particularly concerned with community guidelines. The sayings of Jesus found in it are perhaps a later insertion.

31 This is almost identical with Matthew 7.6, but here the proverb stands alone.

32 This and the following saying occur in Paul (1 Thessalonians), but were clearly considered as sayings of Jesus.

It is easier for a rope to go through the eye of a needle than for a rich man to enter the kingdom of God.[26]

—FREER MS VARIANTS TO MARK 10.25 AND PARALLELS

Do not allow us to be led into temptation.[27]

—CYPRIAN, DE DOMINICA ORATIONE 7

Who can make wine from thorns, or wheat from thistles?[28]

—DIALOGUE BETWEEN CHRIST AND THE DEVIL

Do not let the sun go down on your prayer.[29]

—DIALOGUE OF ADAMANTIUS 13

But love those who hate you and you will not have an enemy.[30]

—DIDACHE 1.3

Do not give what is holy to the dogs.[31]

—DIDACHE 9.5

The final day comes like a thief in the night.[32]

—DIDYMUS, DE TRINITATE

33 This and the preceding saying occur in Paul (1 Thessalonians), but were clearly considered sayings of Jesus. Since Paul's writings precede this source (by a few centuries) it is historically more likely that they originated with Paul but became absorbed into the body of Jesus sayings. Yet it is not impossible that Paul was quoting a saying of Jesus originally.

✦ Didymus the Blind was a fourth-century church father in the tradition of Origen. Despite going blind at the age of four he was brilliantly learned.

34 Stoning was a punishment for blasphemy. The people who would punish someone for blasphemy, Jesus thinks, are the same people who would end up as interpreters of his teaching. In the Gospel of Thomas saying 13, Jesus tells Thomas three things. Thomas tells Simon, Peter, and Matthew that if he utters even one of the things they will stone him.

✦ Ephrem was a fourth-century Syrian church father. His commentary on the Diatessaron is an important witness to a now-lost gospel harmony that merged all four of the canonical gospels into a single narrative. He was also a prolific poet.

35 This is reported as third-person speech in the original. I have converted it to first person.

36 The implication of this is that Jesus existed before the earth was created, and that his followers were preelected.

37 In the Gospel of Thomas saying 2 and its parallels, trouble or suffering is one of the stages that leads to the kingdom.

✦ The Epistle of Barnabas is a letter from the late first or early second century.

38 "I am" sayings occur in a variety of cultures. Jesus's "I am" sayings are particularly associated with the Gospel of John. The beautiful saying here is unparalleled in Christian literature.

It will not come at night, so that the day should overtake you in darkness.[33]

—DIDYMUS, DE TRINITATE

The doctor runs to where the sickness is. I go to the stone-throwers because they will become interpreters instead of stone-throwers.[34]

—EPHREM, COMMENTARY ON THE DIATESSARON 17.1

How long shall I be with you and bear you? This generation is abhorrent to me. They tried me, ten times, but these have done so twice ten, twenty times.

—EPHREM, COMMENTARY ON THE DIATESSARON 17.6

I will cleanse the house of my kingdom of every source of sin.[35]

—EPHREM, COMMENTARY ON THE DIATESSARON 18.7

I chose you before the earth was created.[36]

—EPHREM, COMMENTARY ON THE DIATESSARON 4.18

Those who want to see me and touch my kingdom must receive me through distress and suffering.[37]

—EPISTLE OF BARNABAS 7.11B

I am hope for the hopeless, the helper of the helpless, the treasure of the needy, the doctor of the sick, the resurrection of the dead.[38]

—EPISTULA APOSTOLORUM 21

◆ The Epistula Apostolorum, or Epistle of the Apostles, is probably from the second century and represents an early Christian orthodox point of view.

39 Taken by itself, this saying is quite puzzling. In the Epistula Apostolorum, the disciples agree and ask Jesus whether he is speaking in parables. Jesus explains that he means that not only will the disciples be saved, but also their own disciples will have the hope of salvation.

40 Christian imagery can be overfamiliar to anyone who has sung hymns or attended church. Yet these are extraordinary, extravagant images—shining seven times brighter than the sun, borne on wings of clouds!

41 In the Gospel of Peter, these are the last words of Jesus before he dies, and are an interesting variation on "My God, My God … ," the words from Psalm 22 that Jesus quotes in the Gospel of Matthew.

◆ The Gospel of Peter is a second-century production that J. D. Crossan has argued is based on a lost document named by him the Cross Gospel. Although many scholars remain unconvinced, Crossan asserts that the Cross Gospel was independent of the canonical accounts of the Passion.

42 In Matthew 27.52–53, the graves open up once Jesus has died.

◆ Hippolytus of Rome lived in the third century. His Refutation of All Heresies provides much important, though biased, information on Gnosticism and other nonorthodox forms of early Christianity.

43 This Judas is "Judas the Betrayer," not Judas Thomas.

And we asked him, "Teacher, do we have a single hope of the inheritance as well as them?"

He replied and said to us, "Are the fingers of the hand unique, or the ears of wheat in the field? Or do all fruit trees give the same fruit? Don't they give fruit according to their nature?"[39]

—EPISTULA APOSTOLORUM 32

Indeed, I tell you, I will come as the shining sun, shining seven times brighter than it, with the wings of the clouds bearing me in glory, and the sign of the cross before me. I will descend to the earth to judge the living and the dead.[40]

—EPISTULA APOSTOLORUM 9

My power, my power, you have forsaken me.[41]

—GOSPEL OF PETER 5.19

Let your Holy Spirit come down and purify us.

—*GREGORY OF NYSSA*, DE DOMINICA ORATIONE 3

The dead will rise up from the graves.[42]

—*HIPPOLYTUS*, REFUTATION OF ALL HERESIES 5.8.23–25

When the Lord described the coming kingdom of the holy, Judas, astonished by the things being said, asked, "And who will see these things?"

The Lord said, "Those who will be worthy will see these things."[43]

—*HIPPOLYTUS*, COMMENTARY ON DANIEL

44 The Docetic heresy viewed Jesus as being simply spirit and even denied that he had any physical manifestation on earth.

✦ Ignatius was bishop of Antioch and died as a martyr in the early second century.

45 This and the following saying emphasize that in any religion or spiritual discipline it is not enough to just pay lip service.

✦ The letter of 2 Clement was not written by Clement of Rome, but is a later second-century text.

46 "Him who after death" is presumably the Devil. The treatment of death here is reminiscent of the Gospel of Thomas. In Thomas saying 60, the lamb can only be eaten if it dies.

47 Although this seems quite straightforward, the interpretation in the letter of 2 Clement tells us that Jesus means that we should keep the flesh pure and the seal (of the covenant?) spotless in order to obtain eternal life. I cannot help feeling that pseudo-Clement is complicating the issue here.

Take hold and touch me and see that I am not a demon without a body.[44]

—IGNATIUS, SMYRNEANS 3.1–2

Not all who say to me, Lord, Lord, will be saved, but only those who act righteously.[45]

—2 CLEMENT 4.2

If you are with me, gathered in my heart, and you do not do my commands, I will throw you out and say to you, "Leave me, I do not know you nor know where you come from, you workers of evil."

—2 CLEMENT 4.5

For the Lord said, "You will be like lambs among wolves." And Peter replied and said to him, "What if the wolves tear apart the lambs?"

Jesus said to Peter, "The lambs should not fear the wolves once they are dead, and you should not be afraid of those who will kill you and cannot do anything more to you. Instead, fear him who after death has power over your body and soul to cast them into burning hell."[46]

—2 CLEMENT 5.2–4

If you have not taken care of the small things, who will give you the great things? For I tell you that whoever is faithful in the smallest is faithful in the greatest.[47]

—2 CLEMENT 8.4–6

48 It has been argued that the original of this saying was in the third person plural. It does seem a little odd if it refers to Jesus. In the Gospel of Thomas saying 38, Jesus says, "Many times you have wanted to hear these words that I say to you, and you had no one to hear them from. The days will come when you will search for me and not find me."

✦ Irenaeus was another of the heresy hunters, who unintentionally preserved for posterity evidence of the very heresies that he was trying to eradicate.

49 A feeling of shame can easily turn into useless guilt, or it can lead to a genuine repentance and transformation in oneself.

✦ The Latin church father Jerome is famous as the translator of the Bible into Latin.

50 Justin Martyr quotes a few versions of Jesus's sayings that have significant differences from the canonical versions that we know.

✦ Justin Martyr was a second-century church father born in Palestine as a pagan.

51 The influence of God is seen as a chain extending from God to Jesus ("the one who sent me") to whoever hears Jesus. This reminds me somewhat of the chain of inspiration that, according to Plato's Ion, extends from the Muse to the poet to the reciter of poetry to the listener.

52 The image of hidden treasure occurs regularly in early Christianity, and, at least in this case, the treasure is interpreted as a spiritual state, not as some vague future reward.

53 Christianity in the second century, when Justin Martyr lived, was a maelstrom of conflicting loyalties and doctrines. Justin Martyr's loyalties would now be called proto-orthodox.

Often when I desired to hear one of these words I had
no one to say it to me.[48]

—IRENAEUS, AGAINST HERESIES 1.20.2

There is a shame that leads to death and a shame that
leads to life.[49]

—JEROME, COMMENTARY ON EZEKIEL TO EZEK 16.52

For whoever hears me and practices the things I tell
him hears the one who sent me.[50]

—JUSTIN, APOLOGY 1.16.10

Whoever hears you hears me, and whoever rejects you
rejects me, and whoever rejects me rejects the one
who sent me; and whoever hears me, hears the one
who sent me.[51]

—JUSTIN, APOLOGY 1.16.10

Where the mind is, there is the treasure.[52]

—JUSTIN, APOLOGY 15.16

Many will appear in my name, outwardly closed in
sheep's skins, but inwardly they are ravening wolves.[53]

—JUSTIN, DIALOGUE 35.3

54 Lewis Carroll, the author of the Alice books, commented in his preface to *Sylvie and Bruno*, "Be sure the safest rule is that we should not dare to live in any scene in which we dare not die."

◆ The Liber Graduum, the Book of Steps or Book of Stages, consists of thirty sermons written in fourth-century Syria. Quotations from Jesus are dotted throughout the text, and many of them do not identifiably come from the New Testament gospels.

55 These are very tough demands to be made on anyone. Asceticism was strong in Syrian Christianity, though the Liber Graduum is not the product of a monastic community.

56 The reference to events and characters in Jesus's life mark this and the next saying as secondary. The saying that mentions Iscariot is presumably a postresurrection saying, because it must be considered as being said after Judas Iscariot betrayed Jesus.

There will be divisions and schisms.

—JUSTIN, DIALOGUE 35.3

Many false Christs and false apostles will arise and will lead astray the faithful.

—JUSTIN, DIALOGUE 35.3

In whatever circumstances I find you, that is how I will judge you.

—JUSTIN, DIALOGUE 47.5

As you are found, so will you be taken up.[54]

—LIBER GRADUUM 3.3, 15.4

Men who do not have wives and women who do not belong to men resemble angels and cannot die. Whoever does not leave his wife and children and family, and everything he owns in the land, will not be worthy of me.[55]

—LIBER GRADUUM 19.14

I have not come to judge the world, but to teach them in humility and to save them, and to create an example for my disciples, so that they will do as I do.

—LIBER GRADUUM 2.2

Whoever does not wash the feet of his enemies—as I did to Iscariot—because he knows that they are going to betray him to death, is not worthy of me.[56]

—LIBER GRADUUM 2.4.6

57 This saying is strangely at odds with the ascetic qualities of many of the Liber Graduum sayings, although if one is sexually abstinent and possesses no property, one has little to fear from prostitutes and tax collectors.

58 The Muslim Jesus also has the ascetic characteristics and distrust of the world that the Jesus of the Syrian sayings has. There may be a connection between the Syrian traditions and the Muslim Jesus.

59 The images derive from Hellenistic athletic tradition, much as in 2 Timothy 4.7, "I have fought the good fight, I have finished the race, I have kept the faith."

Everyone who does not walk in my footsteps and does not enter the houses of tax-collectors and whores and teach them as I have indicated, will not be perfect.[57]

—Liber Graduum 2.6.2

Be patient and pray for them [evil people] so that they might have life. If they repent, then, look, they will be ashamed of their weaknesses and will come to you and have life. But if they don't repent, remaining in their evil, take comfort in this, that on the judgment day I will reveal myself in glory, and you will be glorified with me before all creation, and they will be humbled before me and before all creation, both the things above and the things below. But you must not rejoice in their ruin, but pray for them so that they might be raised up.

—Liber Graduum 20.13

Be humble and holy, and separate from the world and from marriage, and love all people, and follow me. Do not be of the world, for I was neither in it, nor worked in it. But follow me and be perfect.[58]

—Liber Graduum 25.4

After you have been struck and beaten, you will have won, and you will rise up from the contest, and receive the wreath, and depart from the world with this prize. Then your weaknesses will not be recalled, but as you are found in victory, so will you be taken up, adorned with your wreath.[59]

—Liber Graduum 3.3

60 In a twist on this famous saying, the reason why one should not throw pearls before swine—offer teaching to those who do not wish or deserve it—is that one will weaken one's own faith by talking to them.

61 This seems a very modern psychological assessment of the importance of working with our negative emotions.

62 The word *paraclete* comes from the Greek *parakletos*, someone who comes to one's side.

63 The sayings in the Liber Graduum are often concerned with perfection, the reaching of spiritual maturity.

Whoever does not renounce all that he has, does not take up his cross and follow me, is not worthy of me.

—LIBER GRADUUM 3.5

Whoever does not leave his wife and children and all he has on earth is not worthy of me.

—LIBER GRADUUM 30.25

Do not throw what is holy to the dogs, nor pearls to swine, in case they trample them with their feet and turn and draw you away from your teachings.[60]

—LIBER GRADUUM 30.11

Anyone who curses, becomes angry, or discovers a weakness in himself, but does not remove it, will not obtain perfection.[61]

—LIBER GRADUUM 4.1

The world cannot hold the Paraclete; the righteous children of this world can only contain the gift of union.[62]

—LIBER GRADUUM 5.18

I will give you perfection, which I will bring about when I come. When I send the Paraclete to the apostles I will also make you perfect because you waited for me and sought the perfection of the angels above, from which your father Adam fell. I will take you and your father Adam back up to the heights from which you have fallen.[63]

—LIBER GRADUUM 9.12

64 Like other extracanonical sayings, this saying states that John the Baptist needed Jesus more than Jesus needed him.

65 No one can truly own nothing in this world, but we can become detached from our possessions.

66 Paul said that we are of the day, not of the night.

67 Perhaps this refers to the money changers in the Temple. This saying crops up dozens of times in Christian literature. It is generally considered to be one of the agrapha that is most likely to be authentic.

✦ Origen was the successor to Clement of Alexandria as head of the catechetical school in Alexandria. He was a brilliant scholar and prolific writer, interpreting scripture allegorically.

68 "To the weak I became weak, so that I might win the weak. I have become all things to all people, that I might by all means save some" (1 Cor. 9.20–22).

Those who are worthy of the resurrection are like the angels of God and cannot die.

—Liber Graduum 15.4

Whoever does not go to anyone who needs him, as I did to John [the Baptist], who needed me, will not be my disciple.[64]

—Liber Graduum 2.4.7

Whoever owns anything is not worthy of me.[65]

—Liber Graduum 3.6

I promised the prophets that I would come and make them perfect.

—Liber Graduum 9.13

I am the day.[66]

—Marcellus from Eusebius, Against Marcellus 1.2

Be skilled money changers.[67]

—Origen, Commentary on John 19.7.2

Because of the weak I was weak, and because of the hungry I was hungry, and because of the thirsty I was thirsty.[68]

—Origen, Commentary on Matthew 13.2

Wisdom sends forth her children.

—Origen, Homilies on Jeremiah 14.5

69 Origen mentions this saying many times in his writings. The idea being expressed is similar to "strive first for the kingdom of God and his righteousness, and all these things will be given to you as well" (Matthew 6.33). If we put our spiritual lives first, then everything else will fit into place.

70 Papyrus Oxyrhynchus 1 is a fragment of an earlier version of the Gospel of Thomas than the Nag Hammadi version. The text is in Greek, the original language of the Gospel of Thomas, whereas the Nag Hammadi version is in Coptic. The "Split the wood" section does not appear in the same place in the Coptic version.

✦ Near the end of the nineteenth century, two British archaeologists, the delightfully named Grenfell and Hunt, supervised the excavation of ancient rubbish heaps in Oxyrhynchus in Egypt. Among the thousands of papyri scraps they found were fragments of lost gospels, including fragments of earlier copies of the Gospel of Thomas than the one found at Nag Hammadi.

71 The last clause doesn't occur in the Coptic version, but it is written on a funeral shroud also found at Oxyrhynchus—Jesus said, "There is nothing buried that shall not be raised up."

72 Papyrus Oxyrhynchus 655 is also a Greek version of the Gospel of Thomas, but a different copy than Papyrus Oxyrhynchus 1 or 654. The first part of this saying matches saying 36 in the Coptic version of the Gospel of Thomas, but the section from "You are much greater" … is absent from it. Clothing can metaphorically refer to one's psychological state—someone who mourns is clothed in sackcloth and ashes, whereas someone in an exalted state is clothed in white garments.

Ask for great things and the small will be given to you; ask for heavenly things and earthly things will be given you.[69]

—ORIGEN, SELECTA IN PSALMS 4.4

Where there are three they are godless. Where there is one alone, I say, I myself am with him. Split the wood and I am there; pick up the stone and you will find me there.[70]

—PAPYRUS OXYRHYNCHUS 1

Recognize what is in front of your face, and what is hidden will be revealed to you. For there is nothing hidden that shall not be revealed, and nothing buried that shall not be raised up.[71]

—PAPYRUS OXYRHYNCHUS 654

Do not care from morning to evening and from evening to morning what food you should eat or what clothing you should put on yourselves. You are much greater than the lilies that neither comb wool nor spin it. When you have no clothing, what will you wear? Who can add to the length of your life? It is he who will give you your clothing.[72]

—PAPYRUS OXYRHYNCHUS 655

… before he does wrong, makes all sorts of clever excuses. But take care that you don't suffer the same things as they do, for the evildoers among men receive their reward not only among the living, but also await punishment and torture.

—PAPYRUS OXYRHYNCHUS 840

✦ These descriptions of Temple purification rites may sound convincing, but are in fact later embellishments. The distinction between external cleanness and internal purity is familiar to us from the canonical Jesus. Although the specific details of ritual washing mentioned here are exotic to us, many churches and synagogues still expect a certain standard of dress, which is the modern equivalent.

73 Similarly in the Gospel of Thomas saying 82, "Whoever is close to me is near to the fire, and whoever is far from me is far from the kingdom."

And he took them and brought them to the place of
purification and walked around in the temple. And a
particular Pharisee, a chief priest named Levi, met them
and said to the savior, "Who allowed you to walk into
this place of purification and to view these holy vessels,
without washing or without your disciples even having
washed their feet? But you have walked into the
Temple unclean, into a place of purity into which no
one walks unless he has washed himself and changed
his garments to look at the holy vessels.

The savior answered and said to him, "Woe to you
blind people, who do not see. You have washed in the
running waters where dogs and pigs have been lying
night and day, and you have bathed and wiped the
outer skin which the whores and flute-girls anoint and
wash and wipe and beautify for the lusts of men; but
inside they are full of scorpions and of all evil. But my
disciples and I, who you say have not bathed, have
been baptized in the waters of eternal life which come
down from heaven.

—Papyrus Oxyrhynchus 840

For whoever is not against you is for you. Whoever is
far away today will be near you tomorrow.[73]

—Papyrus Oxyrhynchus 1224

74 Although Jesus performs healing miracles, and in a few instances his method is described (such as the healing of the man who was blind from birth by using a mixture of spit and mud in John 9.1–7), his sayings are not usually prescriptions! This papyrus fragment is an example of a Christian magical text. Many of these have survived from ancient times. See *Ancient Christian Magic*, edited by Marvin Meyer and Richard Smith, for an extensive collection of these.

75 A very similar passage occurs in 2 Baruch 29.5, a pseudepigraphic work. The exaggerative tone of this passage is quite foreign to the modern mind. A direct line of oral transmission is given for this saying. Papias says that he received it from "John, the follower of the master," who heard it from Jesus.

✦ The works of Papias have survived only in quotation principally by Irenaeus and Eusebius. Papias wrote around the end of the first century and collected the logia of Jesus, emphasizing that he sought out the oral tradition.

Three men came across us in the desert and said to the master Jesus, "What treatment can be given to the sick?"

And he said to them, "I have given olive oil and myrrh for anyone who believes in the name of the Father and the Holy Spirit and the Son."[74]

—PAPYRUS OXYRHYNCHUS 1384

The days will come when vines will grow, each of them having ten thousand branches, and on each branch ten thousand shoots, and on each shoot ten thousand clusters, and on each cluster ten thousand grapes, and each grape when pressed will yield twenty-five measures of wine. And when any of the holy ones takes hold of one of the clusters, another one will cry out, "I am a better cluster, take me, bless the Lord through me." In the same way, a grain of wheat will bring forth ten thousand ears, and every ear will have ten thousand grains, and every grain will give ears, and every ear will have ten thousand grains, and every grain will give five quarts of the best, clean flour; and all the other fruits and seeds and plants in the same proportion, and all animals that use these foods from the earth will be at peace and in harmony with one another, in obedient submission to humanity.[75]

—PAPIAS IN IRENAEUS, AGAINST HERESIES 5.33.3

76 The text is fragmentary so I am grateful to the various academics who have suggested reconstructions of the Greek.

✦ Papyrus Egerton 2 was first published in 1935, having been acquired by the British Museum a couple of years earlier. An additional fragment, Papyrus Köln 255, was found and published in 1987.

77 See also 24 where Jesus tells a man that if he works on the Sabbath knowing what he is doing, then he is blessed.

They came to him to question him, saying, "Teacher Jesus, we know that you have come from God, for what you do puts you above the prophets. So tell us, is it right to give to kings what is owed to them? Should we pay them or not?"

And Jesus, knowing their hearts, was angered and said to them, "Why do you call me teacher with your lips and yet not do what I tell you? Isaiah prophesied correctly of you when he said, 'This people honors me with their lips, but their heart is far from me; in vain they worship me, because they teach doctrines that are human-made commandments.'"[76]

—Papyrus Egerton 2

And Jesus said to the lawyer, "Punish everyone who breaks the law, but not me, for he does not know how he does what he does."[77]

—Codex Bezae addition to Luke 6.4

78 Lepers could not stay in inns, because they were banned from having contact with people who did not have their disease. Various emendations have been suggested to modify the text in line with this.

79 Odes of Solomon 13, "Behold! the Lord is our mirror: open the eyes and see them in Him: and learn the manner of your face."

✦ The works titled "Pseudo-Cyprian" were originally attributed to the church father Cyprian, but are now thought to be written by an anonymous third-century Christian from North Africa.

Then he turned to the rulers of the people and said the following, "Search the Scriptures, for you think that you will have life through them. They bear witness of me. Do not think that I have come to accuse my Father. It is Moses, in whom you put your hope, who accuses you."

And when they said, "We certainly know that God spoke to Moses, but we do not know where you are from," Jesus answered and said, "Now what is being accused is your lack of belief in those who came from him. If you had faith in Moses you would have faith in me, for he wrote about me for your fathers/ancestors."

—PAPYRUS EGERTON 2

Then a leper came to him and said, "Teacher, Jesus, because I traveled with lepers and ate with them in the inn, I became a leper myself. If you wish it, I will be made clean."

The Lord said to him, "I do wish it: be clean." And immediately the leprosy went away from him. Then Jesus said to him, "Go and show yourself to the priest and make an offering for the cleansing, as is commanded by Moses, and sin no more."[78]

—PAPYRUS EGERTON 2

Thus you see me in yourself, as you would see me in water or in a mirror.[79]

—PSEUDO-CYPRIAN, DE MONTIBUS SINA ET SION 13

80 We might deduce that the Holy Spirit is the light that shines within.

81 Although these sound familiar, these antitheses are quite different from the versions found in Matthew's Sermon on the Mount or in Luke. The cause and effect between one's current behavior and future reward is similar to the idea of karma.

82 A "feast of emptiness" is probably a pagan celebration.

✦ The Pseudo-Titus Epistle was wrongly attributed to Titus, the follower of the apostle Paul.

Do not grieve the Holy Spirit which is within you, and do not put out the light that shines within you.[80]

—PSEUDO-CYPRIAN, DE ALEATORIBUS 3

And blessed are those who have hungered and thirsted, for they will be filled there, and woe to those who are full, for they will hunger and thirst there. And blessed are those who have mourned and wept, for they will laugh and be consoled there, and woe to those who are laughing now, for they will mourn and weep unceasingly there. And blessed are those who have been merciful, for they will be shown mercy there, but woe to those who have not been merciful, for they will not be shown mercy.[81]

—PSEUDO-EPHREM, SERMO COMPUNCTORIUS

Woe, woe to the souls that despise their own judgment! I see people whose souls delight themselves vainly and give themselves to the impure world. I see how it is all for the good of the enemy. So I can stand by them and say, "You souls who give yourselves to unchastity and have no fear before God!"

—PSEUDO-TITUS, EPISTLE

What sort of virgin, what sort of woman? What kind of mystery of the resurrection have you shown me, who in the beginning established feasts of emptiness for you and who have taken pleasure in the excesses of the pagans and have taken the same pleasures as they do?[82]

—PSEUDO-TITUS, EPISTLE

83 This is Peter quoting "the Lord" in the Questions of Bartholemew. The Latin and Slavonic versions add "but man the head of woman." This is clearly taken from Paul and turned into a saying of Jesus.

✦ The Questions of Bartholemew was a very popular and rather sensationalist revelation of the workings of heaven and hell. It survives in Latin, Slavonic, and Greek versions.

84 Salome is also present in the Gospel of Thomas saying 61, where she also has a dialogue with Jesus. Clement of Alexandria quotes this extract from the Gospel of the Egyptians in three separate places. Twice, Clement interprets the dialogue literally, "not as if life were bad and creation evil, but as teaching the sequence of nature," and telling us that Jesus "does not speak reproachfully of procreation, for that is necessary for the salvation of believers."

In a third reference to this dialogue, he interprets it figuratively: "Sin is said to be the death of the soul." In this interpretation, "as long as women bear children" means "as long as the desires are active."

✦ The Gospel of the Egyptians is, along with the Jewish-Christian gospel of the Hebrews, a classic "lost gospel," the one that scholars would place at the top of the list of desired texts to be rediscovered. It is probably from second-century Egypt and survives only in quotation by church fathers.

85 Clement quotes this continuation of the exchange between Jesus and Salome only once. Perhaps Jesus refers to emotional bitterness here.

86 This esoteric saying does not appear in the New Testament, but it is widely quoted outside of the canon. William Stroker lists thirteen occurrences of it in various early Christian and Gnostic texts. The earliest of these include the Gospel of Thomas and 1 Clement. In the Gospel of the Egyptians, it is Salome to whom Jesus gives his answer; in the Gospel of Thomas, unnamed disciples. Because of its extensive attestation and parallels to the saying in the writings of Paul, I will stick my neck out here and state that I consider this to be a genuine saying of Jesus.

Christ is the head of man.[83]

—QUESTIONS OF BARTHOLEMEW 2.6–7

Why do you wonder at the signs? I am giving you a great inheritance that the entire world lacks.

—SYMEON, HOMILY 12.17

Attend to faith and hope through which love of God and love of man is produced, which gives eternal life.

—SYMEON, HOMILY 37.1

When Salome inquired, "For how long will death have power?" the Lord said, "As long as you women bear children."[84]

—THE GOSPEL OF THE EGYPTIANS IN *CLEMENT OF ALEXANDRIA*,
STROMATA 3.6.45

Salome said, "I have done well then in not having borne children."
The Lord answered, "Eat every plant but do not eat the one that contains bitterness."[85]

—THE GOSPEL OF THE EGYPTIANS IN *CLEMENT OF ALEXANDRIA*,
STROMATA 3.9.66

When the Lord was asked when the kingdom would come, he said, "When the two will be one, and the inner as the outer and the male with the female, neither male nor female."[86]

—THE GOSPEL OF THE EGYPTIANS IN *CLEMENT OF ALEXANDRIA*,
STROMATA 3.13.92

87 Theoderet's Church History was written in the fifth century.

88 The life of St. Shenouda is one of the most common Coptic works. Shenouda was an important fifth-century Egyptian monk, the abbot of a desert monastery.

89 The Blickling Homilies were written in Anglo-Saxon and are dated to the ninth or tenth century. These are church sermons for particular days in the Christian calendar. Apocryphal texts are known to have been used in Britain and, particularly, Ireland, and perhaps these sayings are derived from some piece of Apocrypha.

✦ Roderic Dunkerley, the English author of *Beyond the Gospels,* a book from the 1950s that examined the extracanonical literature, has pointed out a few unknown sayings that appear in Old English sermons or homilies.

90 This is not from the Blickling Homilies, but from a twelfth-century English homily in Latin.

Whoever loves the Father also loves the Son, who was brought forth from him.[87]

—THEODERET, CHURCH HISTORY 1.4.45

Truly your eye will never be closed in eternity for the light of the world.[88]

—VITA SCHNUDI

When you see growing and blowing all the fruits of the earth, and the fragrant odors exhaling from plants, then soon afterwards they shall dry up and dwindle away on account of the summer's heat.[89]

—BLICKLING HOMILIES

You have me ever present among believing people, through the glory of my divine nature.

—BLICKLING HOMILIES

Judge now, as you would that you will be judged hereafter at the last day of this world.

—BLICKLING HOMILIES

You need not be sad nor troubled in your hearts, for I will intercede for you with the Father, that he may preserve you through his heavenly power.

—BLICKLING HOMILIES

I will not leave you without a leader but I will send you the Paraclete.

—BLICKLING HOMILIES

Be brave in war, and fight with the old serpent, and you will receive an everlasting kingdom.[90]

—OLD ENGLISH LATIN HOMILY

Jewish Sayings

☐ Introduction to the Jewish Sayings

Jesus was Jewish, and Christianity sprang up within Judaism. As far as we know, all of Jesus's immediate disciples were Jewish, and the very earliest Christianity existed as a sect within Judaism. But within a matter of years, Gentiles were joining the movement. The subsequent relaxing of some of the Jewish ritual requirements for Gentile converts loosened the sect's Jewish moorings, and Christianity floated off as a separate religion. By the time the Gospel of John was written at the end of the first century, "the Jews" had become the antagonists in the story, even though the author of that gospel is generally considered to be Jewish. On the Jewish side, the *Birkat Ha Minim* prayer of the late first century incorporated antiheretical material. With the destruction of the Temple in 70 C.E. and the expulsion of Jews from Judaea in 135 C.E., Judaism underwent massive changes as it adapted to its new situation and developed into Rabbinical Judaism, creating a new culture and literature. The compilation of the massive Talmuds codified the religious practices of Rabbinical Judaism.

Despite the development of Christianity into an entirely separate religion, Jewish forms of Christianity survived for several centuries. Jewish Christians were ethnically Jewish and still considered themselves to be Jews. They eventually found themselves between two faiths, belonging to neither, considered heretics both by Jews and by the newly emergent orthodox Christianity. Though Jewish Christianity survived as distinctive sects well beyond the adoption of Christianity by the Roman emperor Constantine, it was never a large-scale movement and eventually died out. Jewish Christianity is known mostly through its surviving literature. The Gospel of the Hebrews, the Gospel of the Nazareans, and the Gospel of the Ebionites are known mainly through quotations by the church fathers, though a few readings from these gospels survive in medieval Christian Bible manuscripts. Jewish Christians took issue with the influence of the apostle Paul, and the Pseudo-Clementine Recognitions and Homilies are interpreted as referring to Simon Magus as a cipher for Paul.

The Talmud is the preeminent collection of Rabbinical Judaism. It consists of the Mishnah, a third-century collection of Rabbinical wisdom and interpretation of law organized into tractates, and the Gemara, the subsequent tradition of commentary and interpretation that grew around the Mishnah. The two compilations of the Babylonian and Palestinian Talmuds are huge and fascinating collections of commentary and counter-commentary on aspects of Jewish law and practice. Much to the surprise of Christians, references to Jesus in Jewish literature are few and far between, most of them late and satirical. Some see veiled references to Jesus in Rabbinical material concerning Balaam, the strange figure from the biblical book of Numbers; in Ben Stada, a magician who was hung the day before Passover; and, on more solid ground, in ben Pantera, the illegitimate son of a Roman soldier and a Jewish woman named Miriam. This tradition was known to the second-century writer Celsus and indirectly inspired elements of the Monty Python movie *The Life of Brian*.

1 The story of the rich man also appears in Matthew, Mark, and Luke, as well as in this quotation from the church father Origen, and there are significant differences in the words spoken by Jesus in each version. The version given here contains material concerning the poor that is unparalleled elsewhere. Note that the rich man is considered not to have fulfilled Jewish law, so it is not the law itself that is at fault, but the inability of certain Jews, like the rich man, to truly fulfill the intention of the law.

✦ The Gospel of the Nazareans was an Aramaic or Syriac version of the Gospel of Matthew with some expansions and extra material. Little is known of the Nazareans, but they were Jewish Christians in Syria, and their gospel was in use by the second century C.E., and the name for this gospel is due to the modern usage of scholars. Epiphanius wrote of them, "They acknowledged Moses and believed that he had received laws—not this law, however, but some other. And so, they were Jews who kept all the Jewish observances, but they would not offer sacrifices or eat meat. They considered it unlawful to eat meat or make sacrifices with it" (*Epiphanius*, Panarion 1.18).

☐ Jewish Sayings

The other rich man said to him, "Master, what good thing should I do, so that I might live?

He said to him, "Man, do what is in the law and the prophets."

He replied, "I have done that."

He said to him, "Go and sell all that you own, distribute that among the poor, then come and follow me."

But the rich man began to scratch his head and was not pleased. And the Lord said to him, "How can you say, 'I have fulfilled the law and the prophets?' For in the law it is written, 'Love your neighbor as yourself,' and, look, many of your brothers, who are sons of Adam, are clothed with filth and dying of hunger, and your house is full of many good things, and nothing is brought out from it to them."

And he turned and said to his disciple, Simon, who was sitting next to him, "Simon son of Jonah, it is easier for a camel to pass through the eye of a needle than it is for a rich man to enter the kingdom of heaven."[1]

—GOSPEL OF THE NAZAREANS IN *ORIGEN*,
COMMENTARY ON MATTHEW 15.4

2 In the Synoptic Gospels (Mark, Matthew, and Luke), John the Baptist's immersion of Jesus in the Jordan is the beginning of Jesus's ministry. In the Gospel of John, John the Baptist feels that he is unworthy to untie Jesus's sandals, but Jesus tells him that he must act out his role of baptism. In this passage from the Gospel of the Nazareans, Jesus himself considers that he does not need baptism. It appears that Nazarean Jewish Christians were unhappy with the idea of Jesus being baptized by John. Jesus's conflicts with his family set the scene for a number of sayings in the gospels, but his brother James appears as one of the pillars of the Jerusalem church after Jesus's death.

3 Jerome cites this excerpt from the Gospel of the Nazareans in his Dialogue against Pelasgius, concerning the heresy propagated by the Celt Pelasgius, who denied the role of free will. It forms an interesting contrast with the previous excerpt from the Gospel of the Nazareans, in which Jesus does not need to be baptized by John because Jesus has not sinned. Jesus is therefore clearly superior to the prophets.

4 The church father Jerome explains that he found this version of the Lord's Prayer in "the Gospel of the Hebrews," but in this case it is assumed that he meant the Gospel of the Nazareans. In English, this is usually translated as "daily bread," not "bread for tomorrow."

5 The disciples were chosen by Jesus. The Christian doctrine of election states that those who will be saved, or who have the chance of being saved, have already been determined in advance.

Look, the Lord's mother and brothers said to him,
"John the Baptist is baptizing for the remission of sins:
let's go and be baptized by him." But he said to them,
"How have I sinned that I should go and be baptized
by him? Unless what I have said is ignorance?"[2]

—GOSPEL OF THE NAZAREANS IN *JEROME*,
DIALOGUE AGAINST PELASGIUS 3.2

He said, "If your brother has sinned with a word and has
apologized to you, receive him seven times in a day."

His disciple Simon said to him, "Seven times in a day?"

The Lord replied and said to him, "Yes, I tell you,
even as many as seventy times seven times. For in the
prophets too, the word of sin was found, even after
they were anointed with the Holy Spirit."[3]

—GOSPEL OF THE NAZAREANS IN *JEROME*,
DIALOGUE AGAINST PELASGIUS 3.2

Give us this day our bread for tomorrow.[4]

—GOSPEL OF THE NAZAREANS IN *JEROME*,
COMMENTARY ON MATTHEW 6.11

I choose the best for myself: the most worthy are those
whom my Father in heaven has given me.[5]

—GOSPEL OF THE NAZAREANS IN *EUSEBIUS*, THEOPHANY 4.12

6 A version of this also occurs in the Gospel of Thomas and the canonical gospels.

✦ The Ebionites were Jewish Christians who spoke Greek, as did the majority of Jews in the Hellenistic/Roman world, so the Gospel of the Ebionites was written in Greek. The Ebionites rejected the Virgin Birth and were adoptionist, believing that Jesus was adopted as the Son of God at his baptism when the Holy Spirit came down and entered into him. The name *Ebionite* means "the poor."

7 Animal sacrifices were made in the Temple, and the destruction of the Temple meant that sacrifices could no longer be performed. This saying implies that God was thought by the Ebionites to have wanted the sacrifices to end and destroyed the Temple to that effect. The Ebionites were vegetarians, and ancient temples of all religions were full-scale slaughterhouses due to the large number of sacrifices that were required.

8 Although this story is told in the canonical gospels, it does not take the form of a first-person narrative. To the modern reader, this has the curious effect of making the speech seem more fictional, not less.

9 This is also interpreted as a vegetarian response, since the Passover meal involves eating lamb, and an Ebionite Jesus would be a vegetarian. But perhaps Jesus also doesn't wish to eat at the Passover meal because of his impending crucifixion.

10 The Ebionites were also anxious to lessen the importance of John the Baptist. The importance of the baptism was the adoption of Jesus by God as his Son, and John was simply an instrument used to effect this.

It was announced to him, "Look, your mother and brothers are standing outside."

"Who are my mother and brothers?"

He put out his hand to the disciples and said, "Those who do the will of my Father are my brothers and mother and sisters."[6]

—GOSPEL OF THE EBIONITES IN EPIPHANIUS, AGAINST HERESIES 30.14.5

I have come to end the sacrifices, and if you do not cease from sacrifice, the anger of God will not cease from you.[7]

—GOSPEL OF THE EBIONITES IN EPIPHANIUS, AGAINST HERESIES 30.16.5

As I walked along Lake Tiberias, I chose John and James, the sons of Zebedee, and Simon and Andrew and Thaddeus and Simon the Zealot and Judas Iscariot, and it was you, Matthew, I called as you sat at the tax office, and you followed me. Therefore I want you to be twelve disciples as a testimony for Israel.[8]

—GOSPEL OF THE EBIONITES IN EPIPHANIUS, AGAINST HERESIES 30.13.2–3

Where do you want us to prepare the Passover meal for you?

[Jesus said] "Do I really want to eat with you at this Passover?"[9]

—GOSPEL OF THE EBIONITES IN EPIPHANIUS, AGAINST HERESIES 30.22.4

John fell down before him and said, "I beg you, Lord, baptize me."

But he stopped him and said, "Allow it, for it is right that everything should be fulfilled."[10]

—GOSPEL OF THE EBIONITES IN EPIPHANIUS, AGAINST HERESIES 30.13.8

11 This is another saying that is widely attested outside of the canonical gospels, versions of the saying, or elements of it, being found in the Gospel of Thomas, the Book of Thomas the Contender, Pistis Sophia, and the Acts of Thomas.

✦ The Gospel of the Hebrews was written in Greek and is associated with Egypt, where there was an extensive Jewish community. The surviving quotations from the Gospel of the Hebrews have much in common with the sayings material in the Gospel of Thomas and the Synoptic Gospels, and are not specifically concerned with issues regarding Jewish law.

12 In Hebrew and Aramaic, spirit is feminine, and the family unit of the father, mother, and child is a comprehensible trinity. Mount Tabor is in Galilee. In the Apocrypha additions to Daniel, the prophet Habbakuk is taken by an angel by the crown of his head and carried by the hair to the lion's den. The single hair is perhaps a reference to the state of unity.

13 Surely this is as likely to be an authentic saying of Jesus as any, in or out of the New Testament. Christians of all persuasions might be happy to have this as an addition to their canon.

14 James, the brother of Jesus, is an important figure in post-Crucifixion Christianity yet hardly figures in the canonical gospels. James seems to encourage the experience of the risen Lord by vowing not to eat bread until he sees Jesus, perhaps reflecting the ascetic practice of fasting.

The seeker will not stop searching until he finds, and when he has found he will be astonished, and when he has become astonished, he will reign, and once he has reigned he will find rest.[11]

—GOSPEL OF THE HEBREWS IN *CLEMENT OF ALEXANDRIA*, STROMATA 5.14.96

Then the Holy Spirit, my mother, took me by a single hair of my head up to the great Mount Tabor.[12]

—GOSPEL OF THE HEBREWS IN *ORIGEN*, COMMENTARY ON JOHN 2.12

Never be happy, except when you look upon your brother with love.[13]

—GOSPEL OF THE HEBREWS IN *JEROME*, COMMENTARY ON EPHESIANS 3.5

And when the Lord had handed the linen cloth to the priest's servant, he went to James and appeared to him. For James had vowed that he would not eat bread from the time that he drank the cup of the Lord until he would see him risen from among those who sleep. And shortly after, the Lord said, "Bring a table and bread."

He took the bread, blessed it and broke it, and gave it to James the Just and said to him, "Brother, eat your bread, for the Son of Man is risen from among those who sleep."[14]

—GOSPEL OF THE HEBREWS IN *JEROME*, ON ILLUSTRIOUS MEN, 2

15 Here is a balanced view of good and evil, which acknowledges that both good and evil things will happen in the world, but seems to let us choose which of them we are responsible for allowing to pass through us.

✦ The Pseudo-Clementine literature is written in the name of the first-century Clement of Rome, but is in fact fourth-century Jewish Christian. The Homilies are written in Greek and the Recognitions in Latin, and may go back to a slightlier earlier common source. The Pseudo-Clementines are concerned with the adventures of Clement and his contact with the apostle Peter.

16 The Jewish-Christian material frequently mentions the evil one, rather than the Devil or Satan.

17 With no context to make sense of it, we do not know who the sons of Jesus's house are. Are they Christians, or particular Jewish Christians? They are presumably not his family, because "those who do the will of my Father" are his family. However this is interpreted, it does imply a certain exclusivity.

18 The Gospel of John says, "I am the gate; if anyone enters through me, he shall be saved, and shall go in and out, and find pasture" (John 10.9). This non canonical version is more straightforward; the gate of life, which is Jesus, allows us to enter into life.

19 "And the Lord said unto me, 'They have well spoken that which they have spoken; I will raise them up a prophet from among their brethren, like unto thee, and will put my words in his mouth; and he shall speak unto them all that I shall command him'" (Deuteronomy 18.17–18).

20 The deceiver in this context is the apostle Paul, against whom the Pseudo-Clementine literature directs much of its energy. This is obviously an after-the-fact prophecy that represents a particular Jewish-Christian view of the development of Christianity, whereas Paul was responsible for leading Christianity away from Judaism.

It is necessary that good things will come, and blessed is the one through whom they come. And it is also necessary that evil things come, but woe to those through whom they come.[15]

—*Pseudo-Clementine*, Homilies 12.29

Give no opportunity to the evil one.[16]

—*Pseudo-Clementine*, Homilies 19.2.4

My mystery is for me and for the sons of my house.[17]

—*Pseudo-Clementine*, Homilies 19.20

I am the gate of life; whoever enters through me enters into life.[18]

—*Pseudo-Clementine*, Homilies 3.52

I am the one of whom Moses prophesied, saying, "The Lord our God will raise up a prophet for you from your brothers, just as he did me. Hear him in everything, and whoever does not listen to that prophet will die."[19]

—*Pseudo-Clementine*, Homilies 3.53

It is first necessary that a false gospel come through a deceiver, and then, once the holy place is destroyed, the true gospel will be spread in secret to correct the heresies that will come.[20]

—*Pseudo-Clementine*, Homilies 2.17

The evil one is the tempter.

—*Pseudo-Clementine*, Homilies 3.55

21 Rabbi Eliezer, an important second-century figure, was arrested for heresy because he quoted this passage, which was told to him by a Christian. The Christian tells Eliezer that this refers to the question of whether a prostitute's earnings should be used to buy a lavatory for the high priest! This is presumably a satirical reference.

22 The context of this saying is a dialogue between Rabban Gamaliel and a Christian philosopher, who was respected as being wise and just. The Christian is tricked into quoting this saying on one hand, and on the other hand making a decision that contradicts Torah. Whether this is a quotation from an ancient gospel or is just made up for the purposes of the story, the tale reflects ancient competition between Jews and Christians.

23 In this passage, Jesus is summoned from beyond the grave by a necromancer, Onkelos the son of Kalonymos, a nephew of the emperor Titus. It is part of a notorious passage, and we discover that Jesus is being punished by being boiled in excrement, while the Hebrew Bible figure Balaam (sometimes assumed to be a cipher for Jesus) is being boiled in semen. As unpleasant as this is, it is no worse than Canto 28 of Dante's *Inferno*, in which Muhammad is found in the hell of the schismatics, sliced open from chin to crotch, with his internal organs hanging out. These represent low points in the relationships among different religions. Yet Jesus's saying quoted here is rather touching, as if he feels responsible for the wrongs done to Jews by Christians.

24 These words are spoken by Jesus to tell his disciples, "the men of upper Galilee," not to attack the men who are sent to capture him.

✦ The Toledot Yeshu, or Scroll of Jesus, is a medieval Jewish account of the life of Jesus. It is satirical, but still somewhat within the traditional style of rabbinical stories. Jesus is presented as a magician who has illicitly discovered the name of God.

25 In another satirical touch, Jesus lifts his arms like an eagle and flies, using the magic powers given to him by using the ineffable name of God. Judas Iscariot is sent after him, and they have a fight in the air.

"For as the wages of a prostitute she gathered them, and as the wages of a prostitute they shall again be used" (Micah 1.7); it has come from a filthy place and it shall go to a filthy place.[21]

—BABYLONIAN TALMUD, ABODAH ZARAH 17

I came not to take away from the Torah of Moses, but to add to the Torah of Moses.[22]

—BABYLONIAN TALMUD, SHABBATH 116

Seek their good; do not seek their harm. Injuring them is like injuring the apple of your own eye.[23]

—BABYLONIAN TALMUD, GITTIN 57

Wage no battle.[24]

—TOLEDOT YESHU

It is spoken of me, "I will ascend into heaven."[25]

—TOLEDOT YESHU

Gnostic Sayings

☐ Introduction to the Gnostic Sayings

The origins of Gnosticism are shrouded in mystery, and the usefulness of the term itself has been disputed in recent scholarship. The Greek noun *gnosis* means "knowledge," not in a purely intellectual way, but more in the sense of insight or wisdom. Arguments have been made for Gnosticism being a specifically Christian phenomenon; others have argued that it sprang from Jewish roots, and still others that it originated in a pre-Christian pagan form. Yet other scholars wish to treat Gnosticism as a separate religion altogether. There were a great variety of Gnostic groups and sects, and few of these even referred to themselves as Gnostic. The term became widespread when the main sources for Gnosticism possessed by scholars were the works of the heresy-hunting church fathers, such as Epiphanius and Hippolytus. But the label Gnostic, which is by no means an insulting one to the modern mind, has stuck, and despite problems with its definition, we more or less understand what we mean by it.

The discovery of the codices near Nag Hammadi in 1945 and subsequent translation and publication of the texts has opened up our knowledge of Gnosticism. Instead of having to rely on the sarcastic and one-sided accounts of the church fathers, we can read the texts ourselves.

Aside from the Gospel of Thomas, the Nag Hammadi texts that contain the most sayings of Jesus are dialogue gospels. The Dialogue of the Savior, the Apocryphon of James, the Book of Thomas the Contender, and the Gospel of Mary (Gnostic but not part of the Nag Hammadi cache) all contain large sections of dialogue between the disciples and Jesus (often referred to as "the Savior" or "the Lord"). Many of these sayings probably circulated independently as sayings of Jesus before they were put into dialogue form. Alternatively, some of the words ascribed to the disciples may also have been known as Jesus sayings.

While much of the speech attributed to Jesus in the Nag Hammadi writings is extravagant and un-Jesuslike, other sayings have much more in common with the general tradition of Jesus sayings. In ancient times, new writings were often built on the basis of older texts, especially because each new copy of a text was made by hand, and source critics, such as Helmut Koester, have argued that older written traditions lie underneath writings such as the Dialogue of the Savior. Koester thinks that there are a number of first-century sources contained in the Dialogue of the Savior. The number of words attributed to Jesus in the Gnostic material is extensive, so I have selected material that stands on its own. Although I include all of the Jesus sayings from the Gospel of Philip, I have not included absolutely everything in the other sources, and the reader is invited to read the Dialogue of the Savior, the Apocryphon of James, the Book of Thomas the Contender, and the Gospel of Mary in their entirety.

The Gnostics were largely unconcerned with a historical or pseudo-historical Jesus. Gnostic texts contain grand and extravagant cosmological and psychological myths, in which Jesus or some analog of Jesus often plays an important spiritual role. Many of the texts have a Docetic viewpoint. The term *Docetism* derives from the Greek *dokeo*, "to seem," and from this point of view, Jesus was never truly incarnate on earth but was a spiritual being.

1 The Emerald Tablets of Hermes Trismegistus, a Hermetic text, expressed the same truth: "As above, so below."

2 In a sense, one's soul is oneself.

3 In the Gospel of Thomas saying 35, Jesus said, "There is no way that anyone can go into the house of a strong man, unless he binds the strong man's hands; then he can remove him from his house."

4 In the context of the extracts from Theodotus, this is taken to refer to those who will be deceived by the Antichrist.

5 Rest is a common term in Gnosticism and early Christianity. In Genesis, God labored for six days and then had a day of rest. The state of being at rest has some connection with eternity here, because one will rest forever.

✦ The Dialogue of the Savior consists of sayings and discourses of Jesus largely in dialogue with Matthew, Judas (not Iscariot, but probably Judas Thomas, to whom the Gospel of Thomas ascribes its origin), and Mary. The flow of the material is somewhat confused and it is fairly certain that the version we have is based on an earlier version, or upon multiple sayings sources. It was originally in Greek, but we only have the Coptic translation of it contained in Nag Hammadi Codex III.

6 As a redeemer figure, Jesus has opened the way to the Father.

☐ Gnostic Sayings

This realm is modeled after the imperishable realm.[1]

—APOCRYPHON OF JOHN 1.27

Save yourself and your soul.[2]

—CLEMENT, EXCERPTS FROM THEODOTUS 2.2

Bind the body and seize its possessions as if they are those of a strong man who wars against the heavenly soul.[3]

—CLEMENT, EXCERPTS FROM THEODOTUS 52.1

Leave the house of my Father.[4]

—CLEMENT, EXCERPTS FROM THEODOTUS 9.2

The moment has already come, my brothers, to abandon our labor and stand at rest. For whatever stands at rest will rest forever.[5]

—DIALOGUE OF THE SAVIOR 1

But when I came, I opened the way and taught them, the chosen and solitary, the passage through which they will pass.[6]

—DIALOGUE OF THE SAVIOR 1

7 This saying would fit easily into one of the collections of proverbs that are typical of wisdom literature. The importance of the mythical figure Sophia (Wisdom) in Gnostic writings testifies to the influence of the Jewish wisdom tradition on Gnosticism.

8 This is a common saying of Jesus that exists in many versions. It is the mind that lights up the body, but the difference here is that our minds must be in order before this can happen.

9 Seeking and finding, the hidden and the revealed, are also common to Gnostic texts and the material in the canonical gospels. In this saying and the next, the one who seeks or sees also reveals, and the one who speaks also hears. This perhaps reflects a less hierarchical view than in early Christianity, a religious culture where each person was expected both to learn and to teach.

10 There is seemingly a non sequitur in Jesus's answer. Perhaps the darkness and water are within us, just as the spirit is.

For the truth seeks the wise and the righteous.[7]

—DIALOGUE OF THE SAVIOR 7

The lamp of the body is the mind. If the things within you are in order [...] then your bodies are full of light.[8]

—DIALOGUE OF THE SAVIOR 8

His disciples said, "Lord, who is it who seeks and who reveals?"

The Lord said to them, "The one who seeks also reveals."[9]

—DIALOGUE OF THE SAVIOR 9–10

Matthew said to him, "Lord, when I hear [...] and when I speak, who is the one who speaks, and who is the one who hears?"

The Lord said, "The one who speaks also hears, and the one who sees also reveals."

—DIALOGUE OF THE SAVIOR 11–12

"Lord, tell us what existed before heaven and earth came to be." The Lord said, "There was darkness and water and spirit upon the water. And I say to you, what you seek and ask after, look, it is within you."[10]

—DIALOGUE OF THE SAVIOR 15

11 The soul and the spirit were differentiated in ancient times. The soul was one's own, and in most people it looked outward and downward to the things of this world; the spirit was something above one, and, ordinarily, people were not in contact with it. One's soul could look outward to earthly things or upward to the spirit.

12 Having one's own understanding—having a place to put these things in one's own heart—and the ability to follow that understanding—to be able to come out of the world and enter the place of life—is considered fundamental.

13 Gnostic writings can often be quite harsh about the body, but they were not alone in this. Epictetus, the late first-century philosopher, said, "You are a little soul carrying around a corpse."

[…] said, "Lord, tell us where the soul stands and where
the true mind exists."

The Lord said, "The fire of the spirit came into being in
[…] both. Because of this the [soul] came into being and
the true mind came into being within them. If anyone sets
his soul on high, then it/he will be exalted. I tell you,
whoever has power should renounce it and repent. And
let him who [does not] seek and find and rejoice."[11]

—DIALOGUE OF THE SAVIOR 17

Mary asked her brothers, "Where will you put down
the things you ask about the son of Adam?"

The Lord said to her, "Sister, no one can ask about
those things except one who has the place to put them
within the heart and who is able to come out of this
world and enter [the place of life], so as not to be
bound to this impoverished world."[12]

—DIALOGUE OF THE SAVIOR 25

Matthew said, "Lord, I wish to see the place of life,
where there is no evil, but there is pure light."[13]

The Lord said, "Brother Matthew, you cannot see it
while you are carrying around flesh."

Matthew said, "Lord, even if I cannot see it, let me
know it."

The Lord said, "Everyone who has known himself
has seen it in everything given to him to do […] and
he has come to [be like it] in his goodness."

—DIALOGUE OF THE SAVIOR 27

14 It is essential to recognize that one is ordinarily in darkness in order to perceive the light.

15 The "archons," or "rulers," occupy a considerable place in Gnostic literature. They are represented as demonic powers who seek to keep humanity trapped in this world.

16 In the imagery of the Gnostics and the New Testament, one can put on, or wear, different types of garments, which represent different spiritual states. The garments of life are something that Judas does not yet have.

17 This is a nice example of oral transmission: Mary is quoting Jesus. The text adds of Mary, "She spoke this as a woman who had understood perfectly."

In the Dialogue of the Savior and the Gospel of Mary, Mary has a preferential position among the disciples.

Anyone who does not know the [things] of perfection does not know anything. If someone does not stand in the darkness, he will not be able to see the light.14

—DIALOGUE OF THE SAVIOR 34

Judas said, "Look, the rulers exist above us, so they are the ones who will rule over us."

The Lord said, "It is you who will rule them. But when you remove jealousy from yourselves, then you will clothe yourselves with light and enter the bridal chamber."15

—DIALOGUE OF THE SAVIOR 49–50

Judas said, "How will our garments be provided for us?"

The Lord said, "Some will provide them for you, others will receive them [from you....] For it is they who will bring you your garments. For who can reach the place that is the reward? But the garments of life were given to man since he knows the way by which he will depart. And it is difficult even for me to reach it."16

—DIALOGUE OF THE SAVIOR 51–52

Mary said, "So, 'the evil of each day is sufficient' and 'the laborer is worthy of his food' and 'the disciple resembles his master.'"17

—DIALOGUE OF THE SAVIOR 53

[18] It is rather a truism to say that when what is living leaves someone, then that person will be dead, so we must assume that "what is living" refers to the living spirit.

[19] "Woman" is often interpreted metaphorically in the writings of people such as Philo of Alexandria and Clement of Alexandria. John the Baptist is born of woman in the Gospel of Thomas saying 46, but is not part of the kingdom of the Father. Being born of woman refers to the mere biological side of existence, living on earth without any spiritual development. As we have seen, the female character of Mary has a notable role within the Dialogue of the Savior.

[20] Jesus takes Mary's question and approaches it from a completely different point of view. It is not her own personal gain or loss that is significant, but the possibility that she may "reveal the greatness of the redeemer."

Matthew said, "Tell me how the dead die and the living live."

The Lord said, "You have asked me about a saying which eye has not seen, nor even had I heard it except from you. But I will tell you that when what enlivens a person is removed, that person will be called dead. And when what is living departs what is dead, it will not be called alive."[18]

—DIALOGUE OF THE SAVIOR 56–59

The Lord said, "Whatever is born of truth does not die. Whatever is born of woman dies."[19]

—DIALOGUE OF THE SAVIOR 59

Mary said, "Lord, tell me why I have come to this place, to profit from it or to lose?"

The Lord said, "You have come to reveal the greatness of the revealer!"[20]

—DIALOGUE OF THE SAVIOR 60–61

Mary said to him, "Lord, is there a place which [...] lacks truth?"

The Lord said, "That is the place where I am not."

—DIALOGUE OF THE SAVIOR 62–63

21 Again, "rest" is the goal for the Gnostic. The things that will not be able to follow us, our burdens, are probably our worldly attachments and identifications.

22 The answer is something of a non sequitur, indicating that the question is probably secondary, and the saying circulated separately, or was taken from an earlier sayings collection.

Matthew said, "Why can't we rest immediately?"

The Lord said, "You will when you give up these burdens!"

Matthew said, "How does the small unite itself with the great?"

The Lord said, "When you abandon the things that will not be able to follow you, then you will have rest."[21]

—DIALOGUE OF THE SAVIOR 65–68

Mary said, "I want to understand everything, just as it is."

The Lord said, "This is the wealth of those who seek life. For the [...] of this world is [false], and its gold and silver are delusion."[22]

—DIALOGUE OF THE SAVIOR 69–70

His disciples said to him, "What ought we to do so that our work will be perfect?

The Lord said to them, "Be ready before everything. Blessed is the one who has found [...] the struggle [...] his eyes. For he neither killed nor was killed, but came out victorious."

—DIALOGUE OF THE SAVIOR 71–72

Judas said, "Lord, tell me, what is the beginning of the way?"

He said, "Love and goodness. For if one of these existed among the rulers, evil would never have come into being."

—DIALOGUE OF THE SAVIOR 73–74

23 It is the responsibility of the Gnostic to understand, not to accept on faith. The knowing referred to here is the inner knowledge of Gnosis, not intellectual knowledge.

24 This suggests that our aim should be the next step possible for us, the place we can reach, not to try immediately to attain the level of Jesus.

25 The Gospel of Philip 21a says, "Some are afraid that when they arise they will be naked. Because of this, they wish to rise in the flesh, and they do not know that those who wear the flesh are naked themselves. Those who are made into light are stripping themselves naked, they are not being stripped by someone else."

In the saying in the Dialogue of the Savior, it is necessary to be naked so that one is not wearing the impermanent garments of the rulers and the governors.

26 The question refers to the parable of the mustard seed (Mark 4.31–32), which is sown in the earth but grows up so high that the birds of the air can shelter under it. But Jesus's answer has so little connection to Mary's question that the exchange is something like a Zen koan. The mother of everything may be the Holy Spirit or, if the answer has any relationship to the question, the mother of everything might be the earth.

Matthew said, "Lord, you have spoken about the end of everything without worrying."

The Lord said, "You have understood everything I have told you, and you have accepted it on faith. If you have known these things, then they are yours. If you have not, then they are not yours."[23]

—DIALOGUE OF THE SAVIOR 75–76

They said to him, "What is the place we are going to?" The Lord said, "Stand in the place you can reach."[24]

—DIALOGUE OF THE SAVIOR 77–78

Judas said to Matthew, "We want to understand what sort of garments we will be clothed with when we leave the corruption of flesh."

The Lord said, "The rulers and the governors have impermanent garments given only for a short time. But as children of the truth, you should not clothe yourselves with these impermanent garments. I say to you instead that you will become blessed when you make yourselves naked.... "[25]

—DIALOGUE OF THE SAVIOR 84–85

Mary said, "What is the nature of the mustard seed? Is it of heaven or of earth?"

The Lord said, "When the Father established the world for himself, he left much with the mother of everything. Because of this, he speaks and acts."[26]

—DIALOGUE OF THE SAVIOR 88–89

27 The Dialogue of the Savior goes on to give Matthew's comment on this. Matthew said, "When he said 'Pray in the place where there is no woman,' he tells us, meaning, 'Destroy the works of womanhood,' not because there is any other manner of birth, but because they will cease giving birth."

28 Ephesians 6.17 tells us "And take the helmet of salvation, and the sword of the Spirit, which is the word of God."

29 The state of fullness, as opposed to the emptiness of ordinary existence, is known as the *pleroma* in Gnostic terminology.

✦ The Apocryphon of James is in Nag Hammadi Codex I. An *apocryphon* is a secret book, and an alleged letter from James the brother of Jesus frames the rest of the work. It contains a great variety of material, including some simple parables.

30 To be empty is to be drunk; to be full is to be sober. This is a series of dichotomies—opposites—where one can be drunk or sober, awake or asleep, sick or in health.

Judas said, "You have said this to us from the mind of truth. When we pray, how should we pray?"

The Lord said, "Pray in that place where there is no woman."27

—DIALOGUE OF THE SAVIOR 90–91

Judas said, "How is the spirit revealed?"

The Lord said, "How is the sword revealed?"28

—DIALOGUE OF THE SAVIOR 99–100

Truly, I tell you, no one will ever enter the kingdom of heaven at my bidding, but only if you are full yourselves.29

—APOCRYPHON OF JAMES 2.6

The Savior said, "Don't you wish to be filled? And your heart is drunk; don't you want to be sober? So, be ashamed! From now on, awake or asleep, remember that you have seen the Son of Man, and spoken to him, and listened to him. Woe to those who have seen the Son of Man; blessed are those who have not seen the man, and those who have not met with him, and those who have not spoken with him, and those who have not listened to anything he has said; yours is the life. So, know that he healed you when you were sick, so that you might reign. Woe to those who have found ease from their sickness, for they will relapse into sickness. Blessed are those who have not been sick, and who have known relief before falling sick; yours is the kingdom of God. Therefore, I tell you, 'Become full, and leave no place within you empty, otherwise the one who can mock you will come.'"30

—APOCRYPHON OF JAMES 3.3–11

31 This complex and seemingly contradictory set of instructions is resolved by the final sentence. The soul here is equivalent to ordinary human reason, while the spirit is divine. So one should be deficient of the soul and full of the spirit.

Then Peter said, "Look, you have told us, 'Become full' three times, but we are already full."

The Savior replied and said, "Because of this I have told you, 'Become full,' so that you will not be deficient. Those who are deficient will not be saved. For it is good to be full, and bad to be deficient. So, just as it is good that you should be deficient and, on the other hand, bad that you should be full, so whoever is full is deficient, and whoever is deficient does not become full as whoever is deficient becomes full, and whoever has been filled, attains perfection. Therefore, you must be deficient while it is possible for you to be filled, and be full while it is possible for you to be deficient, so that you may be able to fill yourselves to a greater extent. So, become full of the Spirit, but be deficient of reason, for reason belongs to the soul, and is of the soul."[31]

—APOCRYPHON OF JAMES 3.13–18

32 Jesus is saying here that the important thing is to do the will of the Father while one is tempted by Satan, as this would seem to give greater results than at other times.

33 Since Jesus in this speech has already suffered the Crucifixion, this must be a postresurrection speech. This is a difficult speech, listing Jesus's sufferings in a way that has much in common with Paul's boast in 2 Corinthians 11: "Five times I have received from the Jews the forty lashes minus one. Three times I was beaten with rods. Once I received a stoning. Three times I was shipwrecked; for a night and a day I was adrift at sea; on frequent journeys, in danger from rivers, danger from bandits, danger from my own people, danger from Gentiles, danger in the city, danger in the wilderness, danger at sea, danger from false brothers and sisters; in toil and hardship, through many a sleepless night, hungry and thirsty, often without food, cold and naked."

But I replied to him, "Lord, we can obey you if necessary, for we have left our fathers and our mothers and our home villages, and followed you. Let us, therefore, not be tempted by the Devil, who is the evil one."

The Lord answered and said, "What credit is it to you to do the will of the Father if it is not given to you as a gift from him while you are being tempted by Satan? But if you are oppressed by Satan, and persecuted, and you do the will of the Father, I say to you that he will love you, and make you equivalent with me, and will judge you to have become beloved through his providence by your own free will."[32]

—APOCRYPHON OF JAMES 4.1–4

So will you not refrain from loving the flesh and being afraid of suffering? Or don't you know that you have not yet been abused and unjustly accused, and have yet to be locked in prison, and condemned unlawfully, and crucified without cause, and buried as I was myself, by the evil one? Do you expect to spare the flesh, you for whom the Spirit is an enclosing wall? If you ponder how long the world has existed before you, and how long it will continue to exist after you, you will discover that your life is a single day, and your sufferings are a single hour. Since the good will not enter into the world, scorn death, and consider life! Remember my cross and my death, and you will have life!"[33]

—APOCRYPHON OF JAMES 4.5–11

34 It is startling to come across this speech in the midst of all the other material in the Apocryphon of James. In telling his followers to become "seekers of death," Jesus is not just instructing them to meet death without fear, but urging them toward martyrdom.

35 It is hard to believe that Jesus is speaking directly, and not esoterically ("in parables") here, since he tells James that "head" has a specific meaning, and that they do not understand the meaning of "its head was removed."

But I replied and said to him, "Lord, do not mention the cross and your death, for they are far from you."

The Lord answered and said, "Truly, I say to you, no one will be saved unless they believe in my cross. But for those who have believed in my cross, the kingdom of God is theirs. Become seekers for death, like the dead who seek for life, for what they seek is revealed to them. And what is there to trouble them? And for you, when you study death, it will teach you election. Truly, I say to you, no one who fears death will be saved, for the kingdom belongs to those who are dead. Become better than I, become like the son of the Holy Spirit!"[34]

—APOCRYPHON OF JAMES 5.1–6

Then I asked him, "Lord, how can we prophesy to those who ask us to prophesy to them? For many ask us, and want to hear an oracle from us."

The Lord answered and said, "Don't you know that the head of prophecy was cut off with John?"

But I said, "Lord, how can it be possible to remove the head of prophecy?"

The Lord said to me, "When you learn what 'head' means, and that prophecy issues from the head, then you will understand the meaning of 'Its head was removed.' Initially I spoke to you in parables, and you did not understand, now I speak to you openly, and yet you still do not perceive. But, you were a parable of parables for me, and a revelation among revealed things."[35]

—APOCRYPHON OF JAMES 6.1–4

36 Jesus places the focus on our own efforts to be saved.

37 Jesus presents a more psychological way to look at hypocrisy: we have the thought, or the urge to be false, and then act it out.

38 Scholar Helmut Koester explains that female date palms will drop dates unless a male tree is nearby, and the fruit will not germinate. The format of this parable is a classic comparison between the kingdom of heaven and the subject of the parable. Koester thinks that the original parable has been modified several times. The meaning of the parable as we have it is unclear. The initial fruit fell to the ground and withered, but the fruit that was picked was gathered and produced new plants.

39 Even though parables are among the most notable of Jesus's teachings, there are few parables outside of the New Testament and the Gospel of Thomas. This is the second of the parables in the Apocryphon of James. Just before this parable, Jesus gives a list of seven parables known from the New Testament gospels. The parable here is a very straightforward account of nurturing something that has value.

Be eager to be saved without having to be urged.
Rather, be eager on your own, and, if possible, arrive
even before I do; for then the Father will love you.[36]

—APOCRYPHON OF JAMES 6.7

Learn to hate hypocrisy and evil thought; for the
thought gives birth to hypocrisy, and hypocrisy is far
from truth.[37]

—APOCRYPHON OF JAMES 6.8

Do not allow the kingdom of heaven to wither; for it is
like a palm shoot whose dates have fallen around it.
These dates produced leaves, and after they had
sprouted, their productivity dried up. So it is the same
with the fruit which had grown from this root. When
they were picked, they were gathered by many. It was
certainly good, and is it not possible for you to produce
the new plants now, and to find it?[38]

—APOCRYPHON OF JAMES 6.9–12

Be serious about the word. For the first part of the word
is faith, the second, love, the third, works. For from
these comes life. For the word is like a grain of wheat.
When somebody sowed it, he had faith in it; and when
it sprouted, he loved it, because he had seen many
grains in place of one. And when he had worked, he
was saved, because he had prepared it for food, and he
left some of it to sow. So also you can receive the
kingdom of heaven; unless you receive this through
knowledge, you will not be able to find it.[39]

—APOCRYPHON OF JAMES 6.16–18

40 In contrast to the exhortation to martyrdom earlier on, this saying is almost "feel-good!" Jesus's words would not be out of place in a modern self-help guide.

41 This is also a simple and encouraging parable. It does not have the startling twists that are often associated with Jesus's parables.

42 Jesus implies that pride in one's spiritual achievements will nullify them—"turn the kingdom of heaven into a desert within you."

43 Jesus says this in answer to a question of whether matter will be destroyed. This statement of Jesus is not very typical of Gnosticism, in which matter is the lowest level in the hierarchy of soul and spirit.

So, trust in me, my brothers. Understand what the great light is. Even though I go to him, the Father does not need me, for a father does not need a son, but it is the son who needs the father. For the Father of the Son does not need you.

—APOCRYPHON OF JAMES 6.24–26

Listen to the word, understand knowledge, love life, and no one will persecute you or oppress you, other than you yourselves.[40]

—APOCRYPHON OF JAMES 6.27

For the kingdom of heaven is like an ear of grain which sprouted in a field. And when it was ripe, it scattered its fruit and filled the field with ears of grain for another year. You also, do not delay to reap an ear of life for yourselves, that you might be filled with the kingdom![41]

—APOCRYPHON OF JAMES 8.1–4

Do not turn the kingdom of heaven into a desert within you. Do not be proud because of the light that illumines you, but be to yourselves as I am to you. Because of you I have put myself under the curse, that you may be saved.[42]

—APOCRYPHON OF JAMES 8.11–13

All nature, all forms, all creatures exist in and with one another, and they will dissolve again into their own roots. For the nature of matter is dissolved into the roots of its own nature. He who has ears to hear, let him hear.[43]

—GOSPEL OF MARY 2.1–5

✦ The Gospel of Mary was not part of the Nag Hammadi find, but survives in Greek in two small papyrus fragments and most extensively in the Berlin Coptic Codex in a longer version. The Gospel of Mary is a late second-century dialogue gospel.

44 Sin is not a power in itself but is a result of improper union, as is adultery. Later in the Gospel of Mary, the soul is in conversation with powers such as darkness, desire, and ignorance.

45 Once again, the Gnostic Jesus stresses the value of internal, personal experience over external laws and restrictions.

Peter said to him, "Because you have told us everything, tell us this too: What is the sin of the world?"

The savior replied, "Sin does not exist, but you produce sin when you do things that are like adultery, which is itself called sin. For the good came among you to return to its root the essence of every nature. Whoever has a mind to understand, let him understand. Matter gave birth to an unprecedented passion, which grew from something that was against nature. Then a disturbance arises in its entire body. That is why I said to you, 'Be of good courage,' and if you are discouraged, take courage in the presence of the many forms of nature. Whoever has ears to hear, let him hear."[44]

—Gospel of Mary 3.1–9

Peace be with you. Receive my peace. Watch that no one leads you astray, saying, "Look, here! or look, there!" For the Son of Man is within you. Follow him! Those who seek him will find him. Then go and proclaim the gospel of the kingdom. Do not make any laws beyond those I gave you, and do not set a law like the judge does, in case you should be subject to it.[45]

—Gospel of Mary 4.1–10

46 Mary describes her vision in response to a request from Peter. In the noncanonical literature, Peter is often in contention with Mary and the other disciples, but here he acknowledges that Jesus "loved you more than any other woman." The distinction between soul and spirit is common in Gnosticism and in the ancient world in general. Now we are told that there is a third element between soul and spirit—the mind.

47 What Jesus is saying here is akin to the injunction to take care of the small things.

✦ The Book of Thomas the Contender is in Nag Hammadi Codex II, as is the Gospel of Thomas and the Gospel of Philip. "Contender" translates from the Greek *athletes*, "one who struggles," and the Book of Thomas the Contender is quite concerned with struggling with the desires of the body. It is probably from second-century Syria.

48 Light is a metaphor for heightened consciousness in many traditions; witness the term *enlightenment*.

49 The truth is not something that can just be attained and possessed, but must be maintained against "those who wanted to disturb him."

Mary said, I saw the Lord in a vision and I said to Him, 'Lord, today I saw you in a vision.' He answered and said to me, 'Blessed are you who did not waver at the sight of me. For where the mind is, there the treasure is.'

"I said to him, 'Lord, how does someone see the vision, through the soul or through the spirit?'

"The Savior answered and said, 'Not through the soul nor through the spirit, but through the mind that is between the two. That is what sees the vision.'"[46]

—GOSPEL OF MARY 7.1–6

If the things that are visible to you are obscure to you, how can you hear about the things that are not visible? If the deeds of the truth that are visible in the world are difficult for you to perform, how, then, will you perform those that pertain to the exalted height and to the *pleroma* which are not visible? And how will you be called workers? In this respect you are apprentices, and have not yet received the height of perfection.[47]

—BOOK OF THOMAS THE CONTENDER 138.27–35

It is in light that light exists.[48]

—BOOK OF THOMAS THE CONTENDER 139.21

Blessed is the wise man who sought after the truth, and when he found it, rested on it forever and was not afraid of those who wanted to disturb him.[49]

—BOOK OF THOMAS THE CONTENDER 140.40–41

50 Violent, apocalyptic imagery has been typical of Christianity since the beginning.

51 "Woes" are less attractive to the modern mind than beatitudes, because they can seem very judgmental. The wheel that turns in our minds is our turning thoughts. The development of Christian tradition in the Philokalia, the collection of Eastern Orthodox Christian texts, contains a lot of advice on how to work with our turning thoughts.

Hear what I say to you and believe in the truth. The sower and the sown will dissolve in fire, in fire and water, and they will be hidden in dark tombs. And after a long period they will display the fruit of evil trees. They will be punished, killed in the mouth of beasts and men at the urging of the rains and winds and air, and of the light that shines above.⁵⁰

—BOOK OF THOMAS THE CONTENDER 142.9–17

Woe to you godless who have no hope, who rely on things that will not happen!

Woe to you who put your hope in the flesh and in the prison which will perish. How long will you remain oblivious? And how long will you suppose that the unperishing will perish, too? Your hope is set upon this world, and your god is this life. You are destroying your souls.

Woe to you caught in the fire that burns in you, for it cannot be satisfied.

Woe to you because of the wheel that is turning in your minds!

Woe to you within the power of the burning that is in you, for it will devour your flesh openly and secretly tear apart your souls …⁵¹

—BOOK OF THOMAS THE CONTENDER 143.8–20

52 Though these are given as words of Jesus, the basic idea of prisoners bound in a cave comes from Plato's allegory of the cave in Book VII of the Republic. In Plato's account, the prisoners are looking away from the only source of light to the shadow images cast by figures moving behind them.

53 The most obvious facet of Jesus's words here is the depiction of the negative aspects of the human situation. But we are also promised rest, and that we will be able to reign with the King.

Woe to you, prisoners, for you are bound in caves! You laugh, you delight in mad laughter. You do not realize your situation, nor do you know your circumstances, nor understand that you live in darkness and death! Instead, you are drunk with fire and full of bitterness. Your mind is maddened because of the burning that is in you, and the poison and the blows of your enemies are sweet to you. And the darkness rose for you like the light, for you gave up your freedom for slavery. You darkened your hearts and gave up your thoughts to stupidity, and you filled your thoughts with the smoke of the fire within you![52]

—BOOK OF THOMAS THE CONTENDER 143.21–35

Blessed are you who know in advance the difficulties, who flee alien things.

Blessed are you who are reviled and not honored because of the love your Lord has for them.

Blessed are you who weep and are oppressed by the hopeless, for you will be freed from every bondage. Watch and pray that you not come to be in the flesh, but come out of the bondage of the bitterness of this life. And as you pray, you will find rest, leaving behind suffering and disgrace. For when you come out of the sufferings and passions of the body, you will receive rest from the good one, and you will reign with the king. You joined with him and he with you, from now on, forever and ever. Amen.[53]

—BOOK OF THOMAS THE CONTENDER 145.1–15

54 Literally, the father's house would be the Temple in Jerusalem. But the father's house may also be the "house not made of hands," an internal and spiritual "house."

✦ Part of Nag Hammadi Codex II, the Gospel of Philip is an anthology of Valentinian Gnostic material. Valentinus was an influential second-century Gnostic.

55 The Eucharist is the Lord's supper, the partaking of bread and wine that has been part of Christianity since the earliest times. It is possible that the words given here were actually spoken during Valentinian celebrations of the Eucharist. In any case, a second-century version of the Eucharist was very likely to be less formal than the modern developed tradition. Some comparison is being made between, on one hand, the perfect light and the Holy Spirit and, on the other, the angels and the images. There is probably little difference between the perfect light and the Holy Spirit.

56 The disciple is asking Jesus for the wrong thing. In the Gospel of Philip, "mother" often refers to the Holy Spirit, but here it would seem to be one's biological mother.

57 The second-century Infancy Gospel of Thomas contains a similar story with some added words of Jesus: "The Lord Jesus went into the dyer's workshop, took all these cloths and put them into a cauldron full of indigo. When Salem came and saw that the cloths were spoiled, he began to cry aloud and asked the Lord Jesus, saying: 'What have you done to me, son of Mary? You have ruined my reputation in the eyes of all the people of the city; for everyone orders a suitable color for himself, but you have come and spoiled everything.' And the Lord Jesus replied: 'I will change for you the color of any cloth which you wish to be changed,' and he immediately began to take the cloths out of the cauldron, each of them dyed in the color the dyer wished, until he had taken them all out."

Take from every house, gather into the father's house, but do not steal when you are in the father's house, and do not take anything out of the father's house.[54]

—GOSPEL OF PHILIP 16

He says today in the Eucharist, "You who have united the perfect light with the Holy Spirit, unite also our angels with the images."[55]

—GOSPEL OF PHILIP 24

A disciple one day made a request of the Lord for something of this world. He said to him, "Ask your mother, and she will give you what belongs to another."[56]

—GOSPEL OF PHILIP 30

The Lord went into the dying house of Levi. He took out seventy-two colors and threw them into the vat. He brought all of them out white and said, "Thus has the Son of Man come as a dyer."[57]

—GOSPEL OF PHILIP 47

58 This passage, made famous by Dan Brown's novel *The Da Vinci Code*, indicates that Mary is, in this situation, being raised up above the other disciples. The implication is of spiritual superiority, not of an erotic relationship.

59 This saying also occurs in a quotation by the church father Irenaeus: "Fortunate [Blessed] is one who existed before being human," as well as in the Gospel of Thomas 19: "Blessed is he who exists from the beginning before he comes to be."

60 This saying also occurs in the Gospel of Thomas and the Gospel of the Egyptians, but the final section, from "to unite ... " onward, is unique to the Gospel of Philip.

61 In Gnostic writings, there are a number of references to the laughter of Jesus. Jesus's laughter is notably absent in other traditions.

62 The Jesus who speaks this is entirely separate from his body that is dying on the cross. The true Jesus is his spiritual body, not his physical body.

And the companion of the Savior is Mary Magdalene. The Lord loved Mary more than the other disciples and kissed her often on her [mouth]. The rest of them saw him loving Mary and said to him, "Why do you love her more than us?" The Savior replied, "Why do I not love you as I do her? When a blind man and one who can see are both in the dark, they are the same as one another. When the light comes, then he who sees will behold the light and he who is blind will remain in darkness."[58]

—Gospel of Philip 48

Blessed is he who existed before he came into being. For he who exists, did exist and will exist.[59]

—Gospel of Philip 49

I have come to make the below like the above, and the outer like the inner, and to unite them in the place by means of types....[60]

—Gospel of Philip 61

Some attained the kingdom of heaven laughing and rejoiced as they came out of the world. And they came out [...] because [...] a Christian [...][61]

—Gospel of Philip 84

He whom you see on the tree, happy and laughing, is the living Jesus. But the one into whose hands and feet the nails are hammered is his fleshly part, which is the substitute that is being put to shame, the one who came into being in his likeness. But look at him and me.[62]

—Nag Hammadi Apocalypse of Peter

63 "I am" sayings are particularly notable in the canonical Gospel of John. Commentators have often referred to the Gospel of John as "Gnosticising," and in the early second century there was no hard line drawn between Gnostics and other Christians.

+ Hippolytus describes the beliefs of the Naasenes, who he says are named after the serpent Naas, in his Refutation of All Heresies, and this has become known as the Naasene Exegesis.

64 The whitewashed tombs are familiar from Matthew 23.27, but here Jesus reveals that people are tombs if the living one (the Spirit) is not present in them.

65 Hippolytus tells us that this is from the Gospel of Thomas (saying 4), but it is a very different version from the one in our Coptic Gospel of Thomas.

66 This is paralleled in Gospel of Thomas saying 11. What is the answer to this question? Perhaps that the living things will make us alive.

I am the true gate.[63]

—NAASENE EXEGESIS IN *HIPPOLYTUS*, REFUTATION 5.8.20

You are whitewashed tombs, filled inside with the bones of the dead because the living one is not in you.[64]

—NAASENE EXEGESIS IN *HIPPOLYTUS*, REFUTATION 5.8.23–24

Unless you drink my blood and eat my flesh, you will not enter the kingdom of heaven, yet even if you do drink the same cup as the one that I drink, you cannot enter the place where I will be going.

—NAASENE EXEGESIS IN *HIPPOLYTUS*, REFUTATION 5.8.11

Whoever seeks me will find me in children from seven years of age, for in the fourteenth age, I, who was hidden, am revealed.[65]

—NAASENE EXEGESIS IN *HIPPOLYTUS*, REFUTATION 5.7.20

If you ate dead things and made them alive, what will you do if you eat living things?[66]

—NAASENE EXEGESIS IN *HIPPOLYTUS*, REFUTATION 5.8.32

Look, I am here, he who speaks through the prophets, see, I am here.

—*EPIPHANIUS*, AGAINST HERESIES 23.5.5

67 Much like Paul's Christ, who is within—e.g., "We have the mind of Christ" (1 Corinthians 2.14–16)—these words of Jesus tell us that Jesus is an inner spirituality. It is unlikely that the historical Jesus said this, yet he may well have approved of the saying. For a scholarly discussion of early Christianity as a spirit cult, see Stevan Davies's *Jesus the Healer*.

✦ The Gospel of Eve is known only from quotations from Epiphanius, who assigns some quite salacious interpretations to the material, which are just as likely to be the product of his own excited mind.

68 In the Gospel of John chapter 4, Jesus meets the woman of Samaria at the well. Though he refers to living water in his dialogue with her, and though there are many "I am" sayings in the Gospel of John, "I am the living water" does not come directly from that gospel.

✦ Peter of Sicily was a ninth-century Byzantine writer. He wrote *The History of the Manicheans* as an attack on the Paulician sect, which represented a late form of Christian Gnosticism.

My Father still works, and I am working.

—*Epiphanius*, Against Heresies 23.5.5

Father, you begot me, and I came forth from the Father and have come here, and I am in the Father and the Father is in me.

—*Epiphanius*, Against Heresies 69.53.1–2

I knock, and if anyone opens to me, we will enter into him, I and my Father, and make our habitation with him.

—*Epiphanius*, Against Heresies 69.63

I am you and you are I, and in whatever place you are, I am there, and I am sown in everything. And in whatever place you wish, you may gather me, but when you gather me, you gather yourself.[67]

—Gospel of Eve in *Epiphanius*, Against Heresies 26.3.1

I am the living water.[68]

—*Peter of Sicily*, History of the Manicheans 29

Blessed is whoever will dine with me in the kingdom of heaven. You are the salt of the earth and the lamp that lights up the world. Do not sleep or be dormant until you clothe yourselves with the garments of the kingdom, which I have purchased with the blood of grapes.

—Papyrus Berolinensis 22220, Gospel of the Savior 2–4

No portion is greater than your own, nor is any glory more exalted than yours.

—Papyrus Berolinensis 22220, Gospel of the Savior 62

69 Similar to Gospel of Thomas saying 82, this is yet another of those sayings that is widespread outside of the canonical gospels. Its claim to be an authentic saying of the historical Jesus is as good as any.

✦ The papyrus Gospel of the Savior languished unnoticed in the Berlin Museum after it was purchased in 1967. It was eventually noticed in 1991 and translated and published in 1999 by Charles W. Hedrick and Paul A. Mirecki. A further translation and revision of the order was published by Stephen Emmel in 2002 and is included in Bart Ehrman's *Lost Scriptures*. The version here is chiefly paraphrased from Emmel's translation. The Gospel of the Savior contains a large number of speeches by Jesus, but many of them are very fragmentary.

70 Simple and poignant, this resonates with the theme of little children that occurs frequently in the sayings of Jesus.

71 The Pistis Sophia tells us that Jesus spent eleven years conversing with the disciples after he was raised from the dead.

✦ In 1772, A. Askew, a doctor in London, bought the Coptic codex that has become known as Codex Askewianus. We do not know from whom he purchased it. It contains the text of Pistis Sophia, a third-century Gnostic text, the title of which means "Faith-Wisdom."

72 This is a version of the saying found in Gospel of Thomas saying 23. In this context, it at least refers to the rarity of true disciples.

Anyone who comes close to me will be burned. I am
the blazing fire. Whoever is near to me is near the fire,
whoever is far from me is far from life.[69]

— Papyrus Berolinensis 22220, Gospel of the Savior 71

I am with you as a child.[70]

— Papyrus Berolinensis 22220, Gospel of the Savior 73

Rejoice and be glad from now on, for I went to the
places from which I came. From now on I will speak
with you openly from the beginning of the truth to its
completion. From now on I will not hide from you
anything of the height and the place. For to me is given
by the ineffable and the first mystery of all mysteries,
the power to speak to you from the beginning to the
fulfillment and from the inside to the outside and from
the outside to the inside. Listen now, that I may tell
you everything.[71]

— Pistis Sophia

I tell you, one will be found in a thousand, and two in
ten thousand, for the completion of the mystery of the
first mystery.[72]

— Pistis Sophia

73 The Pistis Sopia also assigns an important place to Mary Magdalene. She and John (who is mysteriously referred to as a virgin) will surpass all of Jesus's disciples.

74 Jesus goes on to explain to his disciples that the one who has crucified the world is the one who has found his word and fulfilled it.

✦ The Bruce Codex was bought by James Bruce, a Scotsman, in Upper Egypt around 1769. The Bruce Codex contains the first and second Book of Jeu and an untitled text, both in Coptic. Much of the Books of Jeu is in the dialogue format now familiar in Gnostic writings.

75 The soul is halfway between the earthly body and the divine spirit. The words of Jesus will enable it to become wise and to be liberated from the body.

76 "The middle" is a Gnostic term, particularly used in Valentinian Gnosticism. It often corresponds to the level of the soul, and, as here, often has negative connotations.

But Mary Magdalene and John the virgin will exceed all of my disciples and all of those who will receive mysteries in the ineffable. They will be on my right and on my left, and I am they and they are I, and they will be equal to you in everything, save that your thrones will exceed theirs and my own throne will exceed yours and those of all those who will find the word of the ineffable.[73]

—PISTIS SOPHIA

Blessed is he who has crucified the world and has not let the world crucify him.[74]

—BOOK OF JEU

This is the will of my Father, that you should receive your soul from the generation of the mind and it should cease to be earthly and become wise through what I am telling you in the course of my words, so that you might complete it and be saved from the ruler of this age and his endless traps.[75]

—BOOK OF JEU

Blessed is the one who has known these things. That one has brought down heaven and raised up the earth and has sent it to heaven, and has come to the middle, which is nothing.[76]

—BOOK OF JEU

77 The teaching that Jesus is giving is considered esoteric and should not be divulged for one's personal benefit or to family members.

Preserve these mysteries which I shall give you, and give them to no one except those who are worthy. Do not give them to father or mother or brother or sister or relative, not for food or drink, not for woman, not for gold or silver, nor for anything of this world. Preserve them and do not give them to anyone for the sake of what benefits this world.[77]

—BOOK OF JEU

Islamic Sayings

☐ Introduction to the Islamic Sayings

In 622 c.e. the prophet Muhammad journeyed to Medina in flight from Mecca, and it is from this point that the Muslim calendar begins. Arabia was a Hellenized region, but remote from the great centers of civilization and with no dominant religion. There were different varieties of pagan religion, but also Christian groups, among which were Nestorian Christians, and Jewish groups. Jews and Christians were considered "people of the book" by Muslims, and Moses and other Hebrew Bible figures— and Jesus—were considered prophets of the new faith of Islam.

Jesus appears in the Qur'an a number of times, and some of the words attributed to him in the Qur'an are given here. The speeches of Jesus in the Qur'an passages are unlikely to be derived from any earlier sources, but the account of Jesus's birth, in which Mary gives birth under a palm tree, and the reference to making birds out of clay also appear in the Apocryphal Infancy Gospels. In the Qur'an, as in some Gnostic writings, Jesus himself was not crucified: "They did not kill him and they did not crucify him, but one was made to appear to them like him" (Qur'an 4.154–157).

As Islam developed into a world religion and spread to a variety of cultures, it produced some of the world's great literature, particularly among Sufi writers. In these writings, which are characterized by a mystical approach to God, the figure of Jesus developed in a specifically Islamic way; it is quite a Sufic Jesus that we find in these writings. This was undoubtedly a creative tradition, but we cannot assume that all of the Sufi sayings of Jesus were begotten within Islam. Islamic scholars were hungry for knowledge, and they collected books from all over the known world. Arabic monastic Christianity also contributed to Islamic culture, and it is quite likely that some of the sayings collected here derive from earlier Christian documents. Robert M. Price, in *Deconstructing Jesus*, has put forward a preliminary argument that the sayings contained in al-Ghazali's eleventh- and twelfth-century work *Revival of the Religious Sciences* derive from an existing sayings collection. They display catchword associations of the type found in the Gospel of Thomas and other similar collections.

In Islam, Jesus is a prophet and is not divine, though he is addressed by God in some of the sayings. He is often called Spirit of God, or Word of God, but these are just titles that are not intended to imply any divinity. Although Muslims accept the Virgin Birth, the Muslim Jesus did not die on the cross. The Sufi Jesus is rather ascetic, but an attractive character, humble and eager to learn.

The Islamic material is an embarrassment of riches, and there are more than three hundred sayings or speeches available. What follows is a representative selection of material from the Qur'an and Sufi sources. According to Islamic doctrine, the Qur'an exists only in Arabic and cannot be translated; only its meaning can be translated.

1   A later tradition adds some charming details to the miracle of the table: "He sent down to him a red tray covered with a napkin in which was a broiled fish surrounded by vegetables with the exception of the leek, with salt at its head and vinegar at its tail; and along with it were five loaves on some of which were olives and on the others pomegranates and dates. A great number of people ate of them and they did not diminish; and whenever a diseased person ate of them he was cured. And it was coming down one day and disappearing the next for the space of forty nights" (*Abû al Fidâ* in *Robson*, p. 38).

☐ Islamic Sayings

When the disciples said, "O Jesus, son of Mary, is your Lord able to send down to us a table from heaven?" he said, "Fear God if you are believers." They said, "We wish to eat of it that our hearts may be at rest, and that we may know that you have spoken the truth to us, and that we may be witnesses to it." Jesus, son of Mary, said, "O God, our Lord, send down to us a table from heaven which will be a feast for us, for the first of us and the last of us, and a sign from thee. And give us provision, for thou art the best of providers." God said, "Verily I am sending it down to you, so whoever of you disbelieves afterwards, I will punish him in a way in which I will not punish anyone in the worlds."[1]

—QUR'AN 5.112–115

2 Monotheism, the worship of one God, who alone is divine, is at the foundation of Islam. For Christians, Jesus is divine. The reference to Jesus's mother is more ambiguous. Although Mary is often treated as a goddess in her own right (though she is never referred to as such in Christianity), it is more likely that Jesus's mother in this context is the Holy Spirit, and the Qur'an is referring to the role of Jesus and the Holy Spirit in the Trinity.

3 The prayer assigned to Jesus emphasizes that all of Jesus's miracles were performed in the name of Allah, the only God, and so the miracles do not imply Jesus's divinity.

And when God said, "O Jesus, son of Mary, did you say to men, 'Take me and my mother as gods besides God?'" he said, "Praise be to God! It is not fitting for me to say what is not mine by right. If I had said it thou wouldest have known it; thou knowest what is in my soul, but I do not know what is in thy soul; verily thou art the knower of hidden things. I said to them only what thou commandest me, 'Worship God, my Lord and your Lord,' and I was a witness against them as long as I was among them. If thou punishest them, they are thy servants; and if thou forgivest them, thou art the mighty and the wise one."[2]

—QUR'AN 5.116–118

His prayer by which he was curing the sick and bringing the dead to life was: "O God, thou art the God of those who are in heaven and of those who are on earth; there is no god in them other than thee. And thou art the almighty one of those who are in the heavens and the almighty one of those who are on earth; there is no almighty one in them other than thee. And thou art the King of those who are in the heavens and the King of those who are on earth; there is no king in them other than thee. And thou art the Judge of those who are in the heavens and of those who are on earth; there is no judge in them other than thee. Thy power on earth is like thy power in heaven, and thy authority on earth is like thy authority in heaven. I ask thee by thy noble names. Verily thou art omnipotent.[3]

—THA'LABI, P. 245, IN ROBSON, PP. 34–35

4   In a thoroughly Islamic context, the disciples follow Jesus because he acknowledges that "the Arabian prophet" (Muhammad) is greater than he.

5   The angel Gabriel appeared to Daniel in the Book of Daniel in the Hebrew Bible and to Zaccareus and Mary in the Gospel of Luke. He also has a very important role in Islam, having dictated the Qur'an to Muhammad.

6   This saying and the following saying share the spirit of Gospel of Thomas saying 42, "Be a passer-by." Sufis, like many early Christians, were itinerant, so the two sayings here reflect not just an attitude toward life, but a way of life.

7   Jesus is repeating the classic Sufi message, to be in the world and yet not of it.

8   The body of Jesus sayings has many internal contradictions, since Jesus, in the Islamic tradition as well as in other traditions, is shown as being at ease with sinners and prostitutes.

They [the disciples] were fishermen who were catching fish, and Jesus passed them and said to them, "What are you doing?" They replied, "We are catching fish." He said to them, "Will you not come with me that you may catch men?" They replied to him, "How do you mean?" He said, "We will summon men to God." They replied, "And who are you?" He said, "I am Jesus, son of Mary, God's servant and apostle." They asked, "Is any of the prophets above you?" He replied, "Yes, the Arabian prophet." So those men followed him and believed in him and set out with him.[4]

—*Tha'labi*, p. 245, in *Robson*, p. 35

Jesus asked Gabriel when the Hour was to come. Gabriel answered, "The one you are asking knows no better than the one who asks."[5]

—*Castalani*, Commentary on Bukhari, 1.163.

The world is a place of transition, full of examples; be pilgrims in it, and take warning from the traces of those that have gone before."[6]

—*Jacut's* Geographical Lexicon

Jesus said, "Be in the midst, yet walk on one side."[7]

—*Baidawi*, Commentary on the Koran, p. 71, Constantinople ed.

In the sermons of Jesus, son of Mary, it is written, "Beware how you sit with sinners."[8]

—*Zamakhshari*, Commentary on the Koran, p. 986

9 A fool is the opposite of one who is wise, and the wisdom books of the Hebrew Bible have much to say about fools.

10 There is nothing in this saying that could not go back to Jesus.

11 Most religions have a minimum requirement of external observance. The Gnostics differentiated between *psychics* (those of the soul) and *pneumatics* (those of the spirit).

12 The sayings quoted by al-Ghazali are often concerned with scholars. Sufis were keen to distinguish between book knowledge and spiritual knowledge.

13 In Islam as in Judaism, pigs are unclean animals. The famous saying of not throwing your pearls before swine has less of an impact on Christians because pigs, though considered somewhat dirty, are a source of pork, ham, and bacon, all of which are highly popular in the West.

I have treated the leprous and the blind, and have cured them; but when I have treated the fool, I have failed to cure him.[9]

—EL-LLLUSTATRAF

Whoever knows and does and teaches shall be called great in the kingdom of heaven.[10]

—AL-GHAZALI, REVIVAL OF THE RELIGIOUS SCIENCES, 1.8

God has declared that those who observe the prescribed devotion will be saved, while those who perform worship beyond that, will be drawn close to him.[11]

—AL-GHAZALI, REVIVAL OF THE RELIGIOUS SCIENCES, 1.78

There are many trees, yet not all of them bear fruit; and there are many fruits, yet not all of them are fit for food; and there are many kinds of knowledge, but not all of them are profitable.[12]

—AL-GHAZALI, REVIVAL OF THE RELIGIOUS SCIENCES, 1.26

Do not offer wisdom to those who are not suitable for it, unless you harm it; and do not withhold it from them that are suitable for it, unless you harm them. Be like a gentle physician, who puts the remedy on the diseased spot.

—AL-GHAZALI, REVIVAL OF THE RELIGIOUS SCIENCES, 1.66

Do not hang jewels around the necks of pigs. Wisdom is finer than gems, and those who do not value it, are worse than pigs.[13]

—AL-GHAZALI, REVIVAL OF THE RELIGIOUS SCIENCES, 1.72

14 What was applied to the Pharisees in the gospels is now shifted to the "evil scholars" of Islamic culture. Medieval Islam had a very strong scholastic tradition, but when scholars focus exclusively on intellectual knowledge they can't see the forest for the trees.

15 Although these sayings are scattered throughout al-Ghazali's massive work, when they are extracted in order, there are runs of associations of catchwords and themes that link the passages together.

16 What God is saying to Jesus is probably meant to be attributed to Jesus himself, in the same way that Muhammad is told by God to write down what he dictates.

Evil scholars are like a rock that has fallen at the mouth of a stream; it does not drink the water, yet neither does it let the water flow to the field. And they are like the pipe of a toilet which is plastered outside, and foul inside; or like graves, the outside of which is decorated, while inside are dead men's bones.[14]

—AL-GHAZALI, REVIVAL OF THE RELIGIOUS SCIENCES, 1.49

How can he be a scholar who, when his journey is to the next world, makes for the things of this world? How can he be a scholar who seeks for words in order to communicate by them, and not to act according to them?[15]

—AL-GHAZALI, REVIVAL OF THE RELIGIOUS SCIENCES, 1.50

One who teaches higher knowledge and does not practice its wisdom is like a secret adulteress whose swelling condition betrays her shame. Such a person, who does not act on the precepts he knows, will be shamed by the Lord before all creation on the Day of Judgment.

—AL-GHAZALI, REVIVAL OF THE RELIGIOUS SCIENCES

God said to Jesus, "Exhort yourself, and if you are profited by the exhortation, then exhort others, otherwise be ashamed before me."[16]

—AL-GHAZALI, REVIVAL OF THE RELIGIOUS SCIENCES, 1.52

17 Although a rain miracle might seem quite far from Jesus's original setting, a rough contemporary of Jesus, Honi the Circle-Drawer, from Galilee, is said to have prayed successfully for rain. The prophet Elijah also prayed that rain should cease, and then that it should start again.

18 The Muslim Jesus can be very humble, as shown by this prayer.

If anyone sends away a beggar empty from his house,
the angels will not visit that house for seven nights.

—AL-GHAZALI, REVIVAL OF THE RELIGIOUS SCIENCES, 1.77

It is told that Jesus once went into the desert to pray
for rain. When people gathered round, he said to them,
"Whoever has sinned must go back." Everyone went
away, except one man. Jesus turned to this man and
asked him, "Have you never sinned?" The man replied,
"By God's Name, I know nothing of sin. Indeed, one
day I was saying my prayers, when a woman passed by.
My eye happened to fall upon her, so I plucked it out
and cast it behind her." Jesus then told him to pray. As
soon as he began, clouds proceeded to gather. Rain
began to fall, and it was a good downpour.[17]

—AL-GHAZALI, REVIVAL OF THE RELIGIOUS SCIENCES

The prayer of Jesus: "O God, I am this morning unable
to ward off what I would not, or to obtain what I
would. That power is in another's hands. I am bound by
my works, and there is none so poor that is poorer than
I. O God, do not let my enemy to rejoice over me, nor
my friend to grieve over me; do not let me have trouble
with faith; make the world not be my chief care, and
do not give the power over me to him who will not
pity me."[18]

—AL-GHAZALI, REVIVAL OF THE RELIGIOUS SCIENCES, 1.247

19 Just as many of the Christian sayings ascribed to Jesus are seemingly adaptations of material in the letters of Paul, so too is this adapted from 1 Corinthians 13.1–3, "though I speak with the tongues of men and angels."

20 This is a succinct and vivid admonition against gossip.

God revealed to Jesus, "If you should worship with the devotion of the inhabitants of the heaven and the earth, but do not have love in God and hate in God, it would avail you nothing."[19]

—AL-GHAZALI, REVIVAL OF THE RELIGIOUS SCIENCES, 2.119

Jesus said, "Make yourselves beloved of God by hating the evildoers. Bring yourselves nearer to God by moving further from them, and seek God's favor by their displeasure." They said, "O Spirit of God, then who will we converse with?" Then he said, "Converse with those whose presence will remind you of God, whose words will increase your works, and whose works will make you desire the next world."

—AL-GHAZALI, REVIVAL OF THE RELIGIOUS SCIENCES, 2.119

Jesus said to the apostles, "What would you do if you saw your brother sleeping, and the wind had lifted up his clothing?" They said, "We would cover him up." He said, "No, you would uncover him." They said, "God forbid! Who would do this?" He said, "One of you who hears a word concerning his brother, and adds to it, and relates it with additions."[20]

—AL-GHAZALI, REVIVAL OF THE RELIGIOUS SCIENCES, 2.134

They say that there was no form of address Jesus loved better to hear than "poor man."

—AL-GHAZALI, REVIVAL OF THE RELIGIOUS SCIENCES, 2.154

21 This is a development of the idea that even the Devil can quote scripture for his own purpose. What Satan would gain from getting Jesus to say this is not clear.

22 Sufis had a strong tradition of teacher-pupil relationships, so in this saying it is interesting that Jesus has no teacher.

23 The promised, absent, and unseen pleasure is the afterlife in paradise.

24 This is very ascetic and unlike the Jesus of the gospels, but quite like the outlook of, for instance, the Christian desert fathers, Syrian asceticism, or certain varieties of Sufism. The saying may have been derived from any of these.

When Jesus was asked, "How are you this morning?" he would answer, "Unable to forestall what I hope, or to put off what I fear, bound by my works with all my good in another's hand. There is no poor man poorer than I."

—AL-GHAZALI, REVIVAL OF THE RELIGIOUS SCIENCES, 2.169

Satan, the accursed, appeared to Jesus and said to him, "Say, there is no God but God." He said, "It is a true saying, but I will not say it at your invitation."[21]

—AL-GHAZALI, REVIVAL OF THE RELIGIOUS SCIENCES, 3.25

Jesus lay down one day with his head upon a stone. Satan, passing by, said, "O Jesus, you are fond of this world." So he took the stone and cast it from his head, saying, "Let this be yours together with the world."

—AL-GHAZALI, REVIVAL OF THE RELIGIOUS SCIENCES, 2.169

Jesus was asked, "Who taught you?" He answered, "No one taught me. I saw that the ignorance of the fool was a shame, and I avoided it."[22]

—AL-GHAZALI, REVIVAL OF THE RELIGIOUS SCIENCES, 3.52

Blessed is he who abandons a present pleasure for the sake of a promised one which is absent and unseen.[23]

—AL-GHAZALI, REVIVAL OF THE RELIGIOUS SCIENCES, 3.64

O company of apostles! Make your livers hungry, and bare your bodies; perhaps then your hearts may see God."[24]

—AL-GHAZALI, REVIVAL OF THE RELIGIOUS SCIENCES, 3.65

25   It was said of the Sufi Bahauddin Naqshband, founder of the Nawsh-bandi order, that if a guest visited while he was fasting, he would break his fast to make the guest feel comfortable.

26   These are presumably lecherous glances. Women and men in Islamic societies are expected to dress modestly, in a manner that does not emphasize their sexual nature.

27   Going into silence is another ascetic practice, and one that is not possible as an absolute discipline for anyone involved in everyday life. But it is possible to keep silent at the right time, or to be careful of one's speech.

It is told how Jesus remained sixty days addressing his Lord, without eating. Then the thought of bread came into his mind, and his communion was interrupted, and he saw a loaf set before him. Then he sat down and wept over the loss of his communion, when he beheld an old man close to him. Jesus said to him, "God bless you, you saint of God! Pray to God for me, for I was in an ecstasy when the thought of bread entered my mind, and the ecstasy was interrupted." The old man said, "O God, if you know that the thought of bread came into my mind since I knew you, then forgive me not. No, when it was before me, I would eat it without thought or reflection."[25]

—AL-GHAZALI, REVIVAL OF THE RELIGIOUS SCIENCES, 3.67

Beware of glances; for they plant passion in the heart, and that is a sufficient temptation.[26]

—AL-GHAZALI, REVIVAL OF THE RELIGIOUS SCIENCES, 3.81

Jesus was asked by some men to guide them to some course by which they might enter Paradise. He said, "Do not speak at all." They said, "We cannot do this." He said, "Then only say what is good."[27]

—AL-GHAZALI, REVIVAL OF THE RELIGIOUS SCIENCES, 3.87

Devotion has ten parts. Nine of them consist in silence, and one in solitude.

—AL-GHAZALI, REVIVAL OF THE RELIGIOUS SCIENCES, 3.107

28 A discussion like this between Jesus and John the Baptist is unimaginable outside of the Sufi literature. That one's own anger would provoke God's anger is poetic justice.

29 Pork is unclean for Muslims, as it is for Jews. Jesus is often depicted in the canonical gospels as being fairly unconcerned with ritual purity.

30 This is an interesting question: What is it that God does not know?

31 This saying of Jesus is attributed to one Malik, son of Dinar. The traditions of Muhammad, known as *hadith*, are careful to record the sources of the tradition and its lineage. Dogs do not command a place of respect in Islamic tradition, so the rotting carcass of a dog would be particularly unpleasant.

Whoever lies much loses his beauty; and whoever wrangles with others loses his honor; and whoever is troubled sickens in his body; and whoever is evilly disposed tortures himself.

—*AL-GHAZALI*, REVIVAL OF THE RELIGIOUS SCIENCES, 3.92

John the Baptist asked Jesus what was the most difficult thing to bear. The latter replied, "The wrath of God." "Then," asked John, "what serves most to bring down God's wrath?" "Your own anger," answered Jesus. "And what brings on one's own anger?" asked John. Jesus said, "Pride, conceit, vanity, and arrogance."[28]

—*AL-GHAZALI*, REVIVAL OF THE RELIGIOUS SCIENCES

Jesus, passing by a pig, said to it, "Go in peace." They said, "O Spirit of God, do you speak in that way to a pig?" He answered, "I would not allow my tongue to get accustomed to evil."[29]

—*AL-GHAZALI*, REVIVAL OF THE RELIGIOUS SCIENCES, 3.94

One of the greatest of sins in God's eyes is that a person should say God knows what He does not know.[30]

—*AL-GHAZALI*, REVIVAL OF THE RELIGIOUS SCIENCES, 3.107

Jesus one day walked with his apostles, and they passed by the carcass of a dog. The apostles said, "How disgusting is the smell of this dog!" But Jesus said, "How white are its teeth."[31]

—*AL-GHAZALI*, REVIVAL OF THE RELIGIOUS SCIENCES, 3.108

32 The role of speech, of silence, and of not speaking badly about someone is a strong theme in the al-Ghazali material.

33 This is a variation on a common saying of Jesus.

34 "The world" is not only important in the Sufi sayings, but in the Gospel of John, too: "In the world you will have tribulation, but be of good cheer, for I have overcome the world."

In this and the following sayings, this world is contrasted with the next world. This world is something that we must pass through, but not be attached to.

Christ passed by some of the Jews, who spoke badly of him; but he spoke well to them in return. It was said to him, "Truly these speak badly of you, so why do you speak well to them?" He said, "Each gives out of his store."[32]

—AL-GHAZALI, REVIVAL OF THE RELIGIOUS SCIENCES, 3.134

Take not the world for your lord, unless it takes you for its slaves. Lay up your treasure with him who will not waste it.[33]

—AL-GHAZALI, REVIVAL OF THE RELIGIOUS SCIENCES, 3.151

You company of apostles, truly I have overthrown the world onto her face for you; do not raise her up after me. It is a mark of the foulness of this world that God is disobeyed in it, and that the future world cannot be attained save by abandonment of this one. So, pass through this world, and do not linger there, and know that the root of every sin is love of the world. Often the pleasure of an hour bestows long pain on the one who enjoys it.[34]

—AL-GHAZALI, REVIVAL OF THE RELIGIOUS SCIENCES

He said again, "I have laid the world low for you, and you are seated on its back. Do not let kings and women dispute with you for the possession of it. Do not dispute the world with kings, for they will not offer you what you have abandoned in their world; but guard against women by fasting and prayer."

—AL-GHAZALI, REVIVAL OF THE RELIGIOUS SCIENCES

35 Jesus is personifying the ideal of the wandering itinerant. Poor, wandering monks or the equivalent exist in many cultures, including certain Sufi orders, the Greek Cynics, Buddhist monks, and Franciscan friars.

He said again, "The world seeks and is sought. If a man seeks the next world, this world seeks him till he obtains his full sustenance in it; but if a man seeks this world, the next world seeks him till death comes and takes him by the throat."

—AL-GHAZALI, REVIVAL OF THE RELIGIOUS SCIENCES

The love of this world and of the next cannot agree in a believer's heart, just as fire and water cannot agree in a single vessel.

—AL-GHAZALI, REVIVAL OF THE RELIGIOUS SCIENCES, 3.152

Jesus being asked, "Why don't you take a house to shelter yourself?" said, "The rags of those that were before us are good enough for us."[35]

—AL-GHAZALI, REVIVAL OF THE RELIGIOUS SCIENCES 3.153

36 If one doesn't eat in this world, then one can eat at the bridal feast of Jesus. Fasting in this world (a theme that also appears in the Gospel of Thomas) is not synonymous with literally fasting from food, which is also an important part of Islamic practice.

It is recorded that one day Jesus was troubled by the
rain and thunder and lightning, and began to seek a
shelter. His eye fell upon a tent nearby; but when he
came there, he found a woman inside, and turned away
from it. Then he noticed a cave in a mountain; but
when he came there, there was a lion there. Laying his
hand upon the lion, he said, "My God, you have given
each thing a resting place, but to me you have given
none!" Then God revealed to him, "Your resting-place
is in the abode of my mercy; that I may wed you on the
day of judgment . . . and make your bridal feast four
thousand years, of which each day is like a lifetime in
this present world; so that I may command a herald to
proclaim, 'Where are those who fast in this world?
Come to the bridal feast of Jesus, who fasted in this
world.'"36

—*AL-GHAZALI*, REVIVAL OF THE RELIGIOUS SCIENCES

Ammar ebn Sa'd relates that Jesus arrived at a village
where the inhabitants were all lying dead in the
pathways and around the houses. "O company of
disciples," he declared, "this community has been
destroyed by the wrath of God; otherwise, they would
have been properly buried."

"O Spirit of God," they urged, "let us have news of
what has happened to them!"

So Jesus invoked God's name, and a revelation came,
whereby God told him to call out to the villagers after
nightfall to obtain the answer. When night came, Jesus

37 The fear of hell should be enough motivation for living a simple and ascetic life, according to this story, which is rather less appealing to the modern reader than most of the Islamic Jesus sayings.

went up on a hill and hailed the dead populace, and one of the villagers answered up, "At your service, O Spirit of God!" Jesus asked what had happened to them. The reply came, "We spent a peaceful night and woke up in the morning to find ourselves in the pit of Hell." Jesus asked why. "Because we loved the world," came the answer, "and obeyed the behest of sinful people." "In what way did you love the world?" queried Jesus. "The way a child loves its mother," was the reply. "Whenever it came to, we were happy, and whenever it went away, we became sad and wept." Then Jesus asked, "Why do your comrades not speak up?" "Harsh and brutal angels have clamped red-hot bits on their mouths," the voice answered. "Then how is it you are able to speak?" countered Jesus. "I was not of them," said the other, "even though I was with them. When the torment descended, I remained amongst them. At present, I am at the edge of Hell, not knowing whether I shall be saved or cast down into the infernal depths." At this point Jesus turned to his disciples and told them, "Eating barley bread with rock salt and wearing sackcloth and sleeping on dunghills in squalor is more than enough to assure one's well-being in this world and the next."[37]

—AL-GHAZALI, REVIVAL OF THE RELIGIOUS SCIENCES

38 The waves of the sea are an even worse foundation on which to build a house than the sand of the canonical parable. I am reminded of the epitaph on the gravestone of the English poet John Keats, "Here Lies One Whose Name Was Writ in Water."

39 The rejection of this world, which has been a running theme in the past few sayings, has reached its extreme in this saying. It is more important to abandon this world than to perform good acts in it. Charity is the third pillar of Islam, and in *hadith* (traditional sayings) Muhammad said, "Charity is a necessity for every Muslim." This saying of Jesus flies in the face of this, and this may indicate a pre-Islamic source for the saying (though charity is also important in the Christian tradition).

Woe to him who hath this world, seeing that he must die and leave it, and all that is in it! It deceives him, yet he trusts in it; he relies upon it, and it betrays him. Woe to those who are deceived! When they shall be shown what they loathe, and shall be abandoned by what they love; and shall be overtaken by whatever they are threatened with! Woe to anyone whose care is the world, and whose work is sin; seeing that one day he shall be disgraced by his sin.

—AL-GHAZALI, REVIVAL OF THE RELIGIOUS SCIENCES

Who builds on the waves of the sea? Such is the world; do not take it for your resting-place.[38]

—AL-GHAZALI, REVIVAL OF THE RELIGIOUS SCIENCES, 3.201

Some said to Jesus, "Give us some teaching for which God will love us." Jesus said, "Hate the world, and God will love you."

—AL-GHAZALI, REVIVAL OF THE RELIGIOUS SCIENCES

You company of apostles, be satisfied with a humble portion in this world, so that your faith should be whole. For even as the people of this world are satisfied with a humble portion in faith, so this world should be secured to them.

—AL-GHAZALI, REVIVAL OF THE RELIGIOUS SCIENCES, 3.154

O you who seek in this world to do charity, to abandon it would be more charitable.[39]

—AL-GHAZALI, REVIVAL OF THE RELIGIOUS SCIENCES

40 The idea of a man trying to please two women at once is alien to the Jewish and Christian religious traditions (though not unknown in reality), but of course quite at home in an Islamic context.

41 Of all the Muslim sayings, this is the one that has provoked the most interest as an authentic saying of Jesus. There is no evidence of any bridges having existed in ancient Palestine, and this objection has been raised against the authenticity of the saying. However, there were certainly bridges in the surrounding regions, and it is difficult to believe that there were no makeshift bridges over streams. The saying is carved on the gateway of the mosque at Fatehpur-Sikri, near Agra in India.

42 The techniques of asceticism are often presented in a negative fashion, but here Jesus takes delight in the simplicity of his life.

43 One by one we all end up in the grave, and this is personified by an old hag murdering her husbands. When it is put this way, it is difficult to believe that we allow the petty problems of this life to distract us from our spiritual aims.

The world and the hereafter are like two women which a man is trying to please at the same time; when one is pleased, the other is annoyed.[40]

—AL-GHAZALI, REVIVAL OF THE RELIGIOUS SCIENCES

This world is a bridge. Pass over it. Do not linger upon it.[41]

—AL-GHAZALI, REVIVAL OF THE RELIGIOUS SCIENCES, 4.218

Jesus used to say, "My condition is hunger, my inner garment is fear, and my outer garment wool. I warm myself in the sun in winter; my candle is the moon; my transport is my feet; my food and snacks are the fruits of the earth; neither in the evening nor in the morning have I anything in my possession, yet no one on earth is richer than I."[42]

—AL-GHAZALI, REVIVAL OF THE RELIGIOUS SCIENCES, 3.159

The world was revealed to Jesus in the form of an old woman with broken teeth, with all sorts of ornaments upon her, "How many husbands have you had?" he asked. She said, "I cannot count them." He said, "Have you survived them all, or did they all divorce you?" She said, "No, I have murdered them all." Jesus said, "Woe to your remaining husbands! Why do they not take notice of your former husbands? You have destroyed them one after the other, and yet they are not on their guard against you."[43]

—AL-GHAZALI, REVIVAL OF THE RELIGIOUS SCIENCES 3.161

44 This is a powerful metaphor, and some commentators have proposed that its vivid imagery may go back to Jesus.

45 In this interpretation, walking on water is equated with non-attachment.

Truly I say to you, just as the sick man looks at the food, and does not enjoy it, owing to the extremity of his pain, so the man of this world takes no pleasure in worship, nor does he taste its sweetness for the love he feels of this world. And truly I say to you, that even as a beast, if he is not ridden and exercised, becomes intractable and changes his character, even so, if the heart is not softened by the thought of death, and the fatigue of devotion, it becomes hard and rough. And truly I say to you, just as a bottle, so long as it is not torn or dry, is fit to hold honey, even so the heart, if it is not torn by passion, nor dirtied by desire, nor hardened by comfort, shall become a vessel for wisdom.

—AL-GHAZALI, REVIVAL OF THE RELIGIOUS SCIENCES, 3.161

He that seeks after this world is like one that drinks sea-water, the more he drinks, the thirstier he becomes, until it kills him.[44]

—AL-GHAZALI, REVIVAL OF THE RELIGIOUS SCIENCES

The apostles said to Jesus, "How is it that you can walk upon the water, whereas we cannot?" He said to them, "What do you think of the dinar and the dirham?" They said, "They are precious." He said, "But to me they are equal with the dirt."[45]

—AL-GHAZALI, REVIVAL OF THE RELIGIOUS SCIENCES, 3.175

46 In the Gospel of Thomas saying 76 and its canonical parallels, the treasure that is immune to destruction or decay is not explicitly named.

Jesus said, "There are three dangers in wealth. First, it may be taken from an unlawful source." "And what if it be taken from a lawful source?" they asked. He answered, "It may be given to an unworthy person." They asked, "And what if it be given to a worthy person?" He answered, "The handling of it may divert its owner from God."

—AL-GHAZALI, REVIVAL OF THE RELIGIOUS SCIENCES, 3.178

"Store up for yourselves something which the fire will not devour." They said, "What is that? He answered, "Mercy."[46]

—AL-GHAZALI, REVIVAL OF THE RELIGIOUS SCIENCES, 3.184

You evil scholars, you fast and pray and give alms, and do not what you are commanded, and do not teach what you perform. Your judgment is evil! You repent in words and fantasy, but act according to your lust. It does no good to clean your skins, when your hearts are foul. Truly I say to you, do not be like the sieve, from which the good corn goes out and the husks remain. Even so it is with you, you cause the judgment to issue from your mouths, while the mischief remains in your hearts. You slaves of this world, how shall he win the next world who still lusts after this world, and yearns after it? Truly I say to you, that your hearts shall weep for your actions. You have set the world under your tongues, and good works under your feet. Truly I say to you, you have spoiled your future, and the prosperity of this world is dearer to you than the prosperity of the

47 In Matthew 6.3, Jesus says, "But when you give alms, do not let your left hand know what your right hand is doing." This has a more immediate meaning for Muslims, who eat with the right hand, and enter the mosque with the right foot.

next. Who among mankind is more unfortunate than you, if you only knew it? Woe to you! How long will you describe the path to them that are in earnest, yourselves standing still in one place like those that are bewildered; as though you summoned the inhabitants of the world to leave it to you? Stay, stay! Woe to you! What good does it do for a dark house if a lamp is set on its roof, when everything is dark within? Even so it profits you not that the light of the world should be upon your mouths when your hearts are destitute of it. You slaves of this world, who are neither faithful slaves nor honorable freemen! Soon the world will pull you out by the root, and throw you on your faces, and then your sins will take hold of your hair, and push you from behind, till they hand you over naked and destitute to the royal judge; then He shall show you your wickedness, and make you ashamed of your evil deeds.

—AL-GHAZALI, REVIVAL OF THE RELIGIOUS SCIENCES, 1.198

Jesus told his disciples, "Whenever one of you should fast, he should smear grease on his hair and face and lips, so that no one is aware of his fasting; and when he gives with his right hand, his left hand should not know what his right hand is doing; and when he prays, he should draw a curtain across the doorway; for God gives out his blessings as he portions out his animal feed."[47]

—AL-GHAZALI, REVIVAL OF THE RELIGIOUS SCIENCES

48 God is saying this to Jesus, so it is not strictly a saying of Jesus, but it may as well be coming from Jesus's mouth.

49 The imagery of banging one's head on the roof due to pride instead of humbly kneeling beneath the sheltering roof is pure poetry and very Yeshuine. We have no way of knowing whether this saying precedes its Islamic context, but many of the Islamic sayings capture the voice of the gospel Jesus.

50 The contrast between outward show and inward quality is typical of Jesus's sayings. Who will deny that fashion is intimately connected with personal pride and vanity? The Muslim Jesus states this unequivocally.

51 One would usually consider kings to be less spiritual than monks, but this saying turns this on its head by telling us that the robes of kings should be worn instead of monks' robes. Throughout the ages official priesthoods have been corrupted by their power, and the lustful monk or power-hungry bishop are familiar figures. Here, a king would represent what is truly noble and divine in us.

Blessed is he to whom God teaches His book, and who does not die proud.

—AL-GHAZALI, REVIVAL OF THE RELIGIOUS SCIENCES, 3.256

God revealed to Jesus, "When I bestow a blessing on you, receive it with humble gratitude, that I may lavish upon you my entire bounty."[48]

—AL-GHAZALI, REVIVAL OF THE RELIGIOUS SCIENCES

Christ said, "The reed grows in the plain, but does not grow on the rock. Even so, wisdom works upon the heart of the humble, but does not work upon the heart of the proud. Don't you see, that if a man lifts his head to the roof it wounds him, whereas if he bows down his head the roof shelters him?"[49]

—AL-GHAZALI, REVIVAL OF THE RELIGIOUS SCIENCES, 3.261

Beautiful clothing is pride of heart.[50]

—AL-GHAZALI, REVIVAL OF THE RELIGIOUS SCIENCES, 3.269

Why come you to me with monks' robes on you, while your hearts are the hearts of ravening wolves? Put on the robes of kings, and mortify your hearts with fear.[51]

—AL-GHAZALI, REVIVAL OF THE RELIGIOUS SCIENCES

It is narrated that there was a robber among the children of Israel who had infested the highway for forty years, when Jesus passed by him with a pious Israelite, who was an apostle. The robber said in his heart, "Here is the Prophet of God passing with his apostle by his side; what if I should come out and make

52 Perhaps the robber is intended to be the apostle Paul. Paul was considered an enemy by some of the Jewish Christian groups, and this may have carried into Islam through knowledge of Jewish-Christian texts, such as the Pseudo-Clementine literature.

a third?" Coming out, he tried to approach the apostle, all the while despising himself and magnifying the apostle, and thinking that such as he was not worthy to walk by the side of that righteous man. The apostle perceived him, and said to himself, "Shall such a man walk by my side?" and gathering his skirts together, he went and walked by the side of Jesus, so that the robber remained behind. Then God revealed to Jesus, "Say to them, they must begin their work from the beginning, for I have canceled their previous deeds; I have canceled the good deeds of the apostle for his self-conceit, and the evil deeds of the other for his self-abasement." Then Jesus told them of this, and took the robber for his companion in his pilgrimage, and made him one of his apostles.[52]

—AL-GHAZALI, REVIVAL OF THE RELIGIOUS SCIENCES, 4.120

You company of the apostles fear transgression of the law, but we prophets fear unbelief.

—AL-GHAZALI, REVIVAL OF THE RELIGIOUS SCIENCES, 4.135

You company of apostles, the fear of God and love of Paradise give patience in tribulation and alienate men from the world. Truly I say to you, that eating barley-bread and sleeping with dogs upon a dunghill in the search for Paradise are a small thing.

—AL-GHAZALI, REVIVAL OF THE RELIGIOUS SCIENCES, 4.143

53 While devotion, humility, and prayer obviously require effort, poverty is not usually seen as being the result of hard work. The poverty referred to is the willing poverty of the itinerant, not the unwilling poverty of the helpless poor.

54 In answer to the previous saying, this is a good example of poverty requiring effort.

Christ passed in his wanderings by a man asleep, wrapped in a robe. He woke him, and said, "O you who sleep, rise and make mention of God." He said, "What do you want of me? Truly I have left the world to them that are of the world." He said to him, "Then sleep on, my beloved."

—AL-GHAZALI, REVIVAL OF THE RELIGIOUS SCIENCES, 4.152

Do not look to the wealth of the people of this world; for the glitter of their wealth takes away the light of their faith.

—AL-GHAZALI, REVIVAL OF THE RELIGIOUS SCIENCES, 4.157

Four things can be attained only with hard work— silence, which is the beginning of devotion; humility; constant prayer; and poverty.[53]

—AL-GHAZALI, REVIVAL OF THE RELIGIOUS SCIENCES, 4.173

Jesus used to take with him nothing but a comb and a pitcher. One day, seeing a man comb his beard with his fingers, he cast away the comb; another day, seeing a man drink out of the river with his hands, he threw away the pitcher.[54]

—AL-GHAZALI, REVIVAL OF THE RELIGIOUS SCIENCES, 4.182

Jesus was asked, "Why don't you buy an ass to ride?" He answered, "I am too precious with God for Him to let an ass interrupt my thoughts of Him."

—AL-GHAZALI, REVIVAL OF THE RELIGIOUS SCIENCES, 4.256

55 This could be considered as a healing miracle, since the blind, crippled, paralyzed, disfigured leper is healed by Jesus at the end of the tale. Yet this is not the point of the story. The man is already transformed by his inner knowledge of God, and the return of his health is incidental.

Jesus passed by a man who was blind, leprous, crippled, paralyzed on both sides, and with his flesh scarred from the disease of elephantiasis, but was saying, "Praise be to God, who has kept me free from that with which he has afflicted many of his creatures." Jesus said to him, "Sir, what form of affliction is that which has been kept away from you?" He answered, "O Spirit of God, I am better off than those into whose hearts God has not put that knowledge of himself which he has put into mine." Jesus said, "You have spoken truly; give me your hand." He gave his hand, and immediately he became the fairest and best-looking of men, for God had healed him of his afflictions. So he accompanied Jesus, and shared his devotions.[55]

—AL-GHAZALI, REVIVAL OF THE RELIGIOUS SCIENCES, 4.272

Jesus asked the children of Israel, "Where does the seed grow?" They answered, "In the earth." He said, "Truly I say to you, wisdom does not grow except in a heart like that earth."

—AL-GHAZALI, REVIVAL OF THE RELIGIOUS SCIENCES, 4.279

God revealed to Jesus, "When I examine a man's heart, and do not find any love for this world or for the next in it, I fill it with love of me and guard it constantly."

—AL-GHAZALI, REVIVAL OF THE RELIGIOUS SCIENCES, 4.281

Jesus was asked, "What is the best of works?" He answered, "Resignation to God, and love of him."

—AL-GHAZALI, REVIVAL OF THE RELIGIOUS SCIENCES

56 Jesus sounds very Muslim here in referring dubious cases to the developed schools of Islamic law.

They said, "What must we do to be doing the works of God?" Jesus answered them, "This is the work of God, that you believe in him whom he has sent."
—*AL-GHAZALI*, REVIVAL OF THE RELIGIOUS SCIENCES

Blessed is the eye that sleeps and thinks no evil, and wakes to sinlessness.
—*AL-GHAZALI*, REVIVAL OF THE RELIGIOUS SCIENCES, 4.284

The apostles asked Jesus, "What action is just?" He answered, "That of whoever works for God without desiring that anyone should praise him for it."
—*AL-GHAZALI*, REVIVAL OF THE RELIGIOUS SCIENCES, 4.298

Actions are of three sorts—those which are evidently right, which you should pursue; those which are evidently wrong, which you should avoid; and those which are doubtful, which are to be referred to those who know.[56]
—*AL-GHAZALI*, REVIVAL OF THE RELIGIOUS SCIENCES, 4.313

On the authority of Ta'us, "The apostles asked Jesus, 'Is there anyone on earth today like you?'" He answered, "Yes, whoever has prayer for his speech, and meditation for his silence, and tears for his vision, that one is like me."
—*AL-GHAZALI*, REVIVAL OF THE RELIGIOUS SCIENCES, 4.332

57 A well-known Sufi saying, and one that has had some currency in the West, is "This too shall pass." Perhaps Jesus's rather unkind manipulation of the old man illustrates the vicissitude of our thoughts.

58 This is an expansion of Jesus's cry in the Garden of Gethsemane.

59 *The Rubáiyát of Omar Khayyam* expresses a similar sentiment:

> Why, all the Saints and Sages who discuss'd
> Of the Two Worlds so wisely—they are thrust
> Like foolish Prophets forth; their Words to Scorn
> Are scatter'd, and their Mouths are stopt with Dust.
> (Fitzgerald translation, first version, quatrain 25)

It is said that Jesus once sat down by an old man who was digging the earth with a spade. Jesus said, "O Lord God, take away his hope," and the old man put down his spade and lay down. After an hour had passed, Jesus said, "O Lord God, restore hope to him," and he arose, and set about his task. And when Jesus asked him concerning what had transpired he said, "While I was at work my soul said to me, 'How much longer shall you labor, now that you are an old man?' So I cast aside my spade and lay down. Then it said to me, 'By God, you must live out that which is left to you.' So, I arose and took up my spade once more."[57]

—AL-GHAZALI, REVIVAL OF THE RELIGIOUS SCIENCES

Pay no attention to your needs for tomorrow, for if tomorrow is to be part of your lifetime then your needs will come with it, whereas if it is not to be, then you should pay no attention to the lifetimes of others.

—AL-GHAZALI, REVIVAL OF THE RELIGIOUS SCIENCES

You company of apostles, pray to God that this cup may be easy for me; for I fear death with a terror which is like the pains of death.[58]

—AL-GHAZALI, REVIVAL OF THE RELIGIOUS SCIENCES, 4.362

How many a healthy body, a graceful face, and a skillful tongue, will tomorrow be woeful among the levels of Hell![59]

—AL-GHAZALI, REVIVAL OF THE RELIGIOUS SCIENCES

60 No disciple named Joshua is ever mentioned in any other tradition of Jesus. The name Joshua is actually the same name in origin as the name Jesus.

61 Jesus has the title of messiah in Islam, but it is not as significant as it is in Christianity.

62 This is rather a snappy reply from the Jesus who associates himself with sinners and tax collectors.

63 This is sound, practical advice for a wide variety of human endeavors.

The sign by which you are known as being from me is that you love one another.

—*Asin* 130 in *Robson*, p. 54

And Jesus said also to Joshua, his disciples, "As regards the Lord, you must love him with all your heart, then love your neighbor as you love yourself."

They said to him, "Explain to us, O Spirit of God, what is the difference between these two loves, so that we may prepare for them with discernment and clearness." He said, "You love your friend for yourself, and you love yourself for your Lord; so when you guard your friend you do it for yourself, and when you are bountiful yourself, you are so towards the Lord."[60]

—*Asin* 130 in *Robson*, p. 54

The Messiah (God bless him and grant him peace!) passed by some people of the children of Israel, who were weeping, and said to them, "What makes you weep?" They replied, "We are weeping for our sins." He said, "Leave them alone; they are forgiven you."[61]

—*Asin* 119 in *Robson*, p. 52

They saw him coming out of a prostitute's house, then someone said to him, "O Spirit of God, what are you doing with this woman?" He replied, "The doctor comes only to the sick."[62]

—*Asin* 104 in *Robson*, p. 50

Truly, you will obtain what you like only by your patience with what you dislike.[63]

—*Asin* 64 in *Robson*, p. 47

Further Traditions, Fictions, and Forgeries

☐ Introduction to Further Traditions, Fictions, and Forgeries

There are sayings of and writings about Jesus that do not fall into any of the four categories—Christian, Jewish, Gnostic, and Islamic—used in this book. These range from texts from countries that we do not usually associate with Christianity to twentieth- and twenty-first-century productions. The Manichaean religion, which had Gnostic origins and gives an important position to Jesus, spread into countries as widely separated as Spain and China. The Mandaeans also have Gnostic roots and still exist as communities in Iraq and Iran. The Chinese Christian texts that have come to be called the Jesus Sutras have been known to specialist scholars since the early twentieth century, but it is only in the past few years that they have been accessible to nonspecialists. They provide a fascinating view of a form of Christianity that grew up in a culture very different from any other form of Christianity.

Among the scraps of gospels that were discovered in the twentieth century was the Secret Gospel of Mark, allegedly discovered by Morton Smith in the Mar Saba monastery near Jerusalem. Curiously enough, in the Secret Gospel of Mark fragment, Jesus says nothing at all. Stephen C. Carlson's recent book *The Gospel Hoax* demonstrates once and for all that the Secret Gospel of Mark, long a subject of controversy, was a hoax perpetrated by Smith. There have been other academic hoaxes and practical jokes in this area.

As we have seen, there is plenty of little-known material on Jesus, and much of it has surfaced in the past hundred years or so. But curiously, the last century has also seen a number of forgeries of supposedly ancient material. Also, the growth of secular culture has allowed writers to treat the life of Jesus creatively, and so new words have been put into the mouth of Jesus by novelists and other creative writers. Some of the modern creations are acknowledged as fiction from the outset, some are the result of sincerely held beliefs, and others are outright forgeries. None of them offers the original language texts.

1   The correspondence between Jesus and Abgar is a fake that first turns up in the fourth-century church history of Eusebius. Abgar was a first-century king of Edessa in Syria, and Jesus's letter is supposedly in reply to an invitation for Jesus to go to Abgar's court in Syria to heal the king.

Copies of the letter were used in protective magical amulets that were fixed above doors.

2   These speeches by Jesus, called Nbu (Mercury) Christ in the text, might seem quite reasonable in themselves, but in the context of the text they are evidence of Jesus leading some of the Jewish people astray with sorcery and foul rites. The Ginza translates as "treasury" and is one of the Mandaean holy books.

✦   The Mandaeans are the only ancient Gnostics who still survive today. There are Mandaean communities in Iraq and Iran and, through recent immigration, now in North America. They have preserved their traditions, language, and literature. Mandaeans could also be included in the Gnostic section, but the trajectory of their development and our lack of knowledge of their origins leaves them more suited to the further traditions section. John the Baptist is an important figure for the Mandaeans, but he is not treated as being their founder. According to the Mandaeans, Jesus "perverted the Torah" and corrupted the teachings of John the Baptist. This is as dramatic a reversal of the usual attitudes to Jesus as was the Gnostic treatment of the God of the Jewish Bible being the demiurge Yaldabaoth, the ignorant creator of this world.

Further Traditions, Fictions, and Forgeries

Blessed are those who believed in me without having seen me. For it is written of me that those who have seen me will not believe in me, and those who have not seen me will believe and live. But concerning that which you hast written to me, to come to you; it is necessary that I must fulfill all things for which I was sent here, and after fulfilling them should then be taken up to him that sent me. And when I am taken up, I will send you one of my disciples, to heal your affliction and give life to you and those who are with you.[1]

—LETTER OF JESUS TO ABGAR

I am the true God. I have been sent here from my Father. I am the first messenger and the last. I am the Father, the Son, and the Holy Spirit. I came out of the Nazareth.[2]

—THE GINZA

Come and see, I am the one who raises the dead, performs resurrections and deliverances. I am Anosh the Nazorean.

—THE GINZA

3 In the Gospel of Thomas, the kingdom of heaven is also within us and outside of us (Gospel of Thomas saying 3). Many sayings of Jesus in Manichaean literature resemble Gospel of Thomas sayings, and the Gospel of Thomas was undoubtedly used by Manichaeans. There are strong connections between Mani and the ancient city of Edessa in Syria, which has many traditions of the apostle Thomas.

✦ Mani, the founder of the Manichaean religion, was a third-century figure born in Mesopotamia. He acknowledged the Christian, Buddhist, and Zoroastrian religions as divine revelations but felt that they had become corrupted in the course of their transmission. His teaching is often classed as a form of Gnosticism. As a religion, Manichaeism lasted for more than a thousand years, and, though centered in Asia, it spread as far west as France and Spain and as far east as China, leading scholars to class it as a world religion. Manichaean texts, many of which have not yet been published, are in a wide variety of languages, including Coptic. The term *Manichaean* has survived in modern usage as a name for any kind of dualistic doctrine.

4 Jesus is every inch the Eastern sage here.

✦ The Taoist Christian scrolls now known as the Jesus Sutras were discovered in China in 1907 and published in the 1930s, and then forgotten. The Jesus of these texts has become completely Orientalized, but the outlines of his life and aspects of his teaching still have a relationship to the Christian gospels. The texts are dated from the eighth century onward.

5 The Sutra of Jesus Christ consists of a single, long, continuous discourse. This exploration of God being like the wind possibly derives from the ambiguity of the Greek *pneuma*, which can mean both "wind" and "spirit," as in the Gospel of John 3.8: "The wind/spirit blows where it chooses, and you hear the sound of it, but you do not know where it comes from or where it goes. So it is with everyone who is born of the Spirit/Wind."

Look, the kingdom of heaven is within us, and, look, it is outside us. If we believe in it we shall live in it forever.[3]

—MANICHAEAN PSALM BOOK, 160.20–21

Blessed is he who will know his own soul.

—PSALMS OF THOMAS 13.19–20

Repent and I will forgive you your sins.

—MANICHAEAN PSALM BOOK, 239.19–22

Whoever dies will live, whoever lowers himself will be exalted.

—MANICHAEAN PSALM BOOK, 273.10–11

Simon spoke up and said: "We didn't know the truth— and we need salvation."

The Messiah replied: "So, good. Everything that exists needs the True Law. And every kind of person can find what's just below the surface—buried deeper than our eyes."[4]

—THE JESUS SUTRAS: THE THIRD LITURGICAL SUTRA 1.4–6

Nobody has seen God. Nobody has the ability to see God. Truly, God is like the wind. Who can see the wind? God is not still but moves on the earth at all times. He is everything and everywhere.[5]

—THE JESUS SUTRAS: THE FOURTH SUTRA (THE SUTRA OF JESUS CHRIST) 1.5

6 Jesus disowns any claim to messiahship and puts himself in the same position with respect to Muhammad as John the Baptist is to Jesus. But Jesus is accepted as the messiah in Islam, though the term does not carry the same connotations as it does in English.

✦ As we have seen, there is an extensive tradition of Jesus sayings in Islam. These cannot be called fakes any more than the historically uncertain sayings in the canonical gospels can be. But the Gospel of Barnabas is an Islamic fake. It is a medieval creation claiming to be a lost gospel but is very Islamic in its approach to Jesus. It is still very popular in Islam, just as many of the fake writings in this section are still quite popular in the West. We cannot rule out the possibility that the Gospel of Barnabus is drawing on older traditions in places.

Wherefore they sent the Levites and some of the scribes to question him, saying: "Who art thou?"

Jesus confessed, and said the truth: "I am not the Messiah."

They said: "Art thou Elijah or Jeremiah, or any of the ancient prophets?"

Jesus answered: "No."

Then said they: "Who art thou? Say, in order that we may give testimony to those who sent us."

Then said Jesus: "I am a voice that crieth through all Judaea, and crieth: 'Prepare ye the way for the messenger of the Lord,' even as it is written in Esaias."

They said: "If thou be not the Messiah nor Elijah, or any prophet, wherefore dost thou preach new doctrine, and make thyself of more account than the Messiah?"

Jesus answered: "The miracles which God worketh by my hands show that I speak that which God willeth; nor indeed do I make myself to be accounted as him of whom ye speak. For I am not worthy to unloose the ties of the hosen or the ratchets of the shoes of the messenger of God whom ye call 'Messiah,' who was made before me, and shall come after me, and shall bring the words of truth, so that his faith shall have no end."[6]

—GOSPEL OF BARNABUS 42

7   Even though the parable is a form distinctly associated with Jesus, there are few parables in either the extracanonical sayings of Jesus or in Christian literature in general. The parable given here is followed immediately by a very specific interpretation that takes away from the impact of the parable. The servant giving the dregs to his master is the kind of unexpected twist that we expect to see in the parables of Jesus.

In a vessel of the best wine a man gave his enemies to drink so long as the wine was at its best, but when the wine came down to the dregs he gave to his lord to drink. What, think ye, will the master do to his servant when he shall know all, and the servant be before him? Assuredly, he will beat him and slay him in righteous indignation according to the laws of the world.[7]

—GOSPEL OF BARNABUS 111

8 This unusual passage, seemingly modeled after the healing miracles, comes from a collection published by the late-nineteenth- early-twentieth-century German scholar Julius Boehmer. The passage was taken from a recently deceased writer, who claimed to have found it in a Coptic Bible manuscript in the Paris Library. The original has never been found, and it is quite likely a fake.

This episode also pops up in the forged Gospel of the Holy Twelve 21.1–6. See below.

It happened that the Lord went forth from the city and walked with his disciples over the mountain. And they came to a mountain, and the road which led to it was steep. There they found a man with a mule. But the animal had fallen, for the burden was too heavy, and he beat it that it bled. And Jesus came to him and said, "Man, why do you beat your animal? Don't you see that it is too weak for its burden, and don't you know that it suffers pain?" But the man answered and said, "What is that to you? I can beat it as much as I please, since it is my property, and I bought it for a good sum of money. Ask those that are with me, for they know me and know of this." And some of the disciples said, "Yes, Lord, it is as he said." But the Lord said, "Do you not notice how it bleeds, and do you not hear how it laments and cries?" But they answered and said, "No, Lord, we do not hear how it laments and cries." And the Lord was sad and exclaimed, "Woe to you, that you do not hear how it complains to the Creator in heaven, and cries for mercy. But three times woe to him of whom it complains and cries in its distress." And he came forth and touched the animal. And it arose and its wounds were healed. And Jesus said to the man, "Now go and beat it no more, that you also may find mercy."[8]

—Claimed as an extra passage in a Coptic Bible manuscript

9 In many of the sayings of Jesus, both in and out of the canon, Jesus denies his mother and his family. Notovitch's Jesus says the opposite, and launches into an attractive discourse praising woman in her many roles.

✦ Russian journalist Nicolas Notovitch published *The Life of Saint Issa* in the late nineteenth century. *The Life of Saint Issa* is the source of all the speculation about Jesus's lost years in Tibet and India. The book included translations of the supposed texts that Notovitch had found. His work was eventually exposed as fraudulent, but the interest in the lost years of Jesus and his Indian connections has continued.

It is not meet that a son should set aside his mother, taking her place. Whosoever respecteth not his mother, the most sacred being after his God, is unworthy of the name of son.

Listen, then, to what I say unto you: Respect woman, for she is the mother of the universe, and all the truth of divine creation lies in her.

She is the basis of all that is good and beautiful, as she is also the germ of life and death. On her depends the whole existence of man, for she is his natural and moral support.

She gives birth to you in the midst of suffering. By the sweat of her brow she rears you, and until her death you cause her the gravest anxieties. Bless her and worship her, for she is your one friend, your one support on earth.

In the same way, love your wives and respect them; for they will be mothers tomorrow, and each later on the ancestress of a race.

Be lenient towards woman. Her love ennobles man, softens his hardened heart, tames the brute in him, and makes of him a lamb.[9]

—LIFE OF SAINT ISSA 12.9–15

10 For the most part, the Gospel of the Holy Twelve closely paraphrases the canonical gospels. The account of the Lord's Prayer is unusual for its additions such as "the fruit of the living vine" and also for its reference to a combined father-mother parent God.

✦ Reverend G. J. Ouseley claimed that the Gospel of the Holy Twelve was the lost original that lay behind the four gospels, but also that "[the] Gospel of the Holy Twelve was communicated to the Editors, in numerous fragments at different times, by Emmanuel Swedenborg, Anna Kingsford, Edward Maitland, and a priest of the former century, giving his name as Placidus, of the Franciscan Order, afterwards a Carmelite. By them it was as translated from the original, and given to the Editors in the flesh, to be supplemented in their proper places, where indicated, from the 'Four Gospels' (A.V.) revised where necessary by the same." It is claimed to have been preserved by the Essenes, in addition to being the result of something similar to channeling.

The secret of nature is in the hands of God. For the world, before it appeared, existed in the depth of the divine thought; it became material and visible by the will of the Most High.

When you address yourselves to him, become again as children; for you know neither the past, the present, nor the future, and God is the Master of all time.

—LIFE OF SAINT ISSA 11.14–15

But thou, when thou prayest, enter into thy chamber, and when thou hast shut thy door, pray to thy Father-Mother who is in secret; and the secret One that seeth in secret shall approve thee openly.

And when ye pray in common, use not vain petitions, as the heathen do: for they think that they shall be heard for their much speaking. Be not ye therefore like unto them: for your heavenly Parent knoweth what things ye have need of, before ye ask. After this manner therefore pray ye, when ye are gathered together:

Our Parent Who art in heaven: Hallowed be Thy Name. Thy kingdom come. Thy will be done; in earth as it is in heaven. Give us day by day our daily bread, and the fruit of the living vine. As Thou forgivest us our trespasses, so may we forgive the trespasses of others. Leave us not in temptation. Deliver us from evil: for Thine are the kingdom and the power and the glory, forever and ever, Amen.[10]

—THE GOSPEL OF THE HOLY TWELVE 26.4–6

11 Like the Jesus of the Essene Gospel of Peace, this Jesus is also a vegetarian. The Jewish Christian Ebionites were vegetarians, and saying 6 in the Jewish Sayings section (page 61) also condemns animal sacrifice.

12 In a charming elaboration of the fishing metaphor common in the canonical gospels, the net contains crabs, lobsters, sharks, and creeping things. But the author of *The Aquarian Gospel of Jesus the Christ* forgot that shellfish, including crabs and lobsters, are unclean food for Jews.

✦ *The Aquarian Gospel of Jesus the Christ* was first published in 1907. It does not claim to have been taken from a previously unknown manuscript, but was dictated from the Akashic records, a theosophical forerunner of channeling. Jesus has once again been to India during his lost years. And Tibet. And Persia, Assyria, Greece, and Egypt. *The Aquarian Gospel of Jesus the Christ* is quite a massive work, and much longer than any other gospel, though a good deal of it adapts from and expands on the canonicals.

13 Little in the ancient sayings of Jesus, whether Christian, Gnostic, or Muslim, is as explicit in its explanation of the kingdom as this is.

It came to pass one day as Jesus had finished his discourse, in a place near Tiberias where there are seven wells, a certain young man brought live rabbits and pigeons, that he might have to eat with his disciples.

And Jesus looked on the young man with love and said to him, "Thou hast a good heart and God shall give thee light, but knowest thou not that God in the beginning gave to man the fruits of the earth for food, and did not make him lower than the ape, or the ox, or the horse, or the sheep, that he should kill and eat the flesh and blood of his fellow creatures?"[11]

—THE GOSPEL OF THE HOLY TWELVE 28

Behold, John is a mighty fisher, fishing for the souls of men. He throws his great net out into the sea of human life; he draws it in and it is full.
But what a medley catch! a catch of crabs, and lobsters, sharks, and creeping things, with now and then a fish of better kind.[12]

—THE AQUARIAN GOSPEL OF JESUS THE CHRIST 67.11–12

Behold, indeed, the king has come, but Jesus is not king.
The kingdom truly is at hand; but men can see it not with carnal eyes; they cannot see the king upon the throne.
This is the kingdom of the soul; its throne is not an earthly throne; its king is not a man.[13]

—THE AQUARIAN GOSPEL OF JESUS THE CHRIST 71.2–4

14 *The Essene Gospel of Peace* places great importance on the Earthly Mother as a counterpart of the Heavenly Father. When Szekely wrote this gospel, the Dead Sea Scrolls had not yet been discovered, so knowledge of the Essenes was limited to a few sections of Josephus, Philo, and Pliny.

✦ *The Essene Gospel of Peace* was translated by Edmond Bordeaux Szekely from original Aramaic and Hebrew texts, which he found in the secret library of the Vatican, and which he has unfortunately never been able to produce. *The Essene Gospel of Peace* was first published in German in 1928 and in English in 1937.

15 Szekely's Jesus is a naturist Jesus, healing the sick by getting them to take their clothes off in communion with mother Earth. He is also a vegetarian. Vegetarianism, naturism, and healthy pursuits such as hiking were very typical of the 1920s and 1930s, particularly in Germany, where Szekely's works were initially published. Fortunately, there are no anti-Semitic elements—also a distinctive aspect of the 1920s and 1930s—within the Essene writings of Szekely, which allows for their enduring appeal.

16 This doesn't read like any of the ancient traditions of Jesus, but it makes sense in terms of modern spiritual teachings.

Your Mother is in you, and you in her. She bore you; she gives you life. It was she who gave to you your body, and to her shall you one day give it back again. Happy are you when you come to know her and her kingdom, if you receive your Mother's angels and if you do her laws. I tell you truly, he who does these things shall never see disease. For the power of our Mother is above all. And it destroys Satan and his kingdom, and has rule over all your bodies and all living things. The blood which runs in us is born of the blood of our Earthly Mother. Her blood falls from the clouds; leaps from the womb of the earth; babbles in the brooks of the mountains; flows wide in the rivers of the plains; sleeps in the lakes; rages mightily in tempestuous seas.[14]

—ESSENE GOSPEL OF PEACE, BOOK ONE

Seek the fresh air of the forest and of the fields, and there in the midst of them shall you find the angel of air. Put off your shoes and your clothing and suffer the angel of air to embrace all your body. Then breathe long and deeply, that the angel of air may be brought within you. I tell you truly, the angel of air shall cast out of your body all uncleannesses which defiled it without and within.[15]

—ESSENE GOSPEL OF PEACE, BOOK ONE

Blessed are the spiritually balanced, for they shall possess knowledge.[16]

—TALMUD OF JMMANUEL 5.5

✦ Purportedly discovered by Billy Meier and a priest in 1963 in the actual cave where Jesus was buried, the original Aramaic scroll was subsequently lost after it had been translated into German and English. UFOs are involved, and there are prophecies concerning modern Israel. Jesus was in India (again). Jesus was not betrayed by Judas Iscariot, who was a loyal disciple and was actually the author of the *Talmud of Jmmanuel*, but by the similarly named Juda Ihariot. Juda Ihariot joined forces with Saul/Paul, who had met Jesus but was chased away by the stick-wielding messiah. The text of the *Talmud of Jmmanuel* is now in its fourth edition.

17 The *Talmud of Jmmanuel* has a discourse directed against "the Israelites." This prophecy is obviously a modern creation by someone who is anti-Israeli.

18 Jesus has a poetic and noble reaction to the news of John the Baptist's execution by Herod. As part of a modern literary work, this excerpt, neither intended as a fake nor a result of traditional religious transmission, has a different feel to anything else attributed to Jesus in the present book.

✦ Kahlil Gibran's book *Jesus, the Son of Man*, first published in 1928, looks at Jesus from the point of view of those who know him. It is a literary work, and in no way intended as a fake, or ever taken that way.

19 Scholar P. R. Coleman-Norton claimed to have discovered this in the library of a mosque in Morocco during the Second World War. It was eventually published, with a full scholarly analysis, as an article in the *Catholic Biblical Quarterly 12*. However, Bruce Metzger, the brilliant text critic, recognized it as a hoax and pointed out that Coleman-Norton used to make exactly the same joke when Metzger attended his lectures.

Two thousand and more years will pass, but meanwhile Israel will never find peace because wars and many calamities will threaten the unlawful occupants of this land; but see to it that nobody leads you astray.[17]

—TALMUD OF JMMANUEL 25.7

And Jesus looked upon him and was troubled, and He said, "What of John?" And the man said, "He was slain this day. He was beheaded in his prison cell." Then Jesus lifted up His head. And then He walked a little way from us. After a while He stood again in our midst. And He said, "The king could have slain the prophet here this day. Verily the king has tried the pleasure of His subjects. Kings of yore were not so slow in giving the head of a prophet to the head-hunters. I grieve not for John, but rather for Herod, who let fall the sword. Poor king, like an animal caught and led with a ring and a rope. Poor petty tetrarchs lost in their own darkness, they stumble and fall down. And what would you of the stagnant sea but dead fishes? I hate not kings. Let them rule men, but only when they are wiser than men."[18]

—JESUS, THE SON OF MAN, CHAPTER 32

"There will be weeping and gnashing of teeth."
"But Rabbi, how can this happen for those who have no teeth?" Whereupon Jesus is said to have replied: "O you of little faith! Do not be troubled. If some have no teeth, then teeth will be provided."[19]

—"AN AMUSING AGRAPHON,"
CATHOLIC BIBLICAL QUARTERLY 12 (1950): 439–449

20 Thaddeus is in the list of twelve disciples, and a Gospel of Thaddeus existed in antiquity. But this particular Gospel of Thaddeus is a modern fake cooked up by Russian academic Yuri Grigoriev as an experiment in producing an apocryphal gospel using modern critical techniques. Much of the gospel consists of variations on the canonical gospels. The section quoted here makes for a very believable noncanonical fragment, though it would hardly set the world alight should it be discovered in Egypt today.

21 In this dialogue, the author is playing on the current interest in Mary Magdalene being Jesus's lover and re-spiritualizing her role.

✦ Jay G. Williams is professor of religious studies at Hamilton College. He has previously written books on Christianity and Buddhism, which have been published by respectable publishers, but this book, *The Secret Sayings of Ye Su: A Silk Road Gospel,* is published via a subsidy press. He describes how a Mr. Wang and a Mr. Chang gave him the manuscript, which, though a Chinese gospel, is written in Koine Greek. His agreement with Wang and Chang did not permit him to publish the original Greek text. *The Secret Sayings of Ye Su* is obviously a hoax, though the surrounding commentary contains a good deal of accurate supporting information. Williams clearly has no malicious motive behind this: he has probably written a Taoist Christian sayings gospel and is seeing how far he can push it.

22 This is a good Buddhist saying, and not too far away from 1 Corinthians 11.2, "Now I praise you, that in all things ye are mindful of me."

Now later that day, as they were passing through the marketplace, Jesus saw traders weighing out cardamom and coriander and cloves for silver and bronze. And he said to them, "See that you give measure for measure. For to him who gives short measure to the poor in this age, shall be given short measure in the age to come. But to him who gives full measure in this age, shall be given abundance in the age to come, and fullness upon fullness."[20]

—GOSPEL OF THADDEUS 57–59

Mary said, "I love you, Ye Su." Ye Su said, "That is a good start; the kingdom is born from love."[21]

—SECRET SAYINGS OF YE SU 11

In all things be mindful.[22]

—SECRET SAYINGS OF YE SU 43

☐ Notes

Introduction

1. The Gospel of Thomas is widely known and, because there are many excellent translations of it, it is outside the scope of this book. I can particularly recommend my own translation in *The Gospel of Thomas: A New Version Based on Its Inner Meaning* (Oregon House, CA: Ulysses Books, 2002) and Stevan Davies's *The Gospel of Thomas: Annotated & Explained* (Woodstock, VT: SkyLight Paths Publishing, 2002).

2. Williams Stroker's *Extracanonical Sayings of Jesus* (Atlanta, GA: Scholars Press, 1989) is the standard modern scholarly collection. It is very useful, but it lacks a lot of the Gnostic material and has no material outside of the Christian/Gnostic/Jewish framework.

3. For instance, chapter 5 in Robert Price's *Deconstructing Jesus* (Amherst, NY: Prometheus Books, 2000).

4. But Stevan Davies has suggested, in his study of early Christianity and spirit possession, *Jesus the Healer* (New York: Continuum, 1995), that the Johannine discourses are the result of Jesus speaking "in the spirit," while the Synoptic sayings tradition is Jesus speaking in a normal state of consciousness.

5. Here I should add that I favor an alternative view, the Farrer hypothesis, which has been gaining some momentum in scholarship as a challenge to the two-source hypothesis. The Farrer hypothesis argues that there are good indications that Luke knew the Gospel of Matthew, hence there is no reason to argue for Q on those grounds.

6. In reply to a query from the author on September 21, 2005, Q specialist William Arnal comments, "While I am convinced that the sayings tradition tends to predate the *biographical* narrative tradition, I do not think this actually requires us to conclude that this earlier tradition is authentic. Certainly my own work on Q and its (apparent) treatment of its oral source material has suggested to me that the ideology of even Q's earliest stage is not already present in the oral tradition; that, instead, the oral tradition was appropriated and opportunistically modified in order to make Jesus a mouthpiece for the views Q's composers wished to purvey."

Suggestions for Further Reading ☐

Barnstone, Willis, and Marvin Meyer, eds. *The Gnostic Bible*. Boston: Shambhala, 2002.

Cameron, Ron, ed. *The Other Gospels: Non-Canonical Gospel Texts*. Philadelphia, PA: The Westminster Press, 1982.

Carlson, Stephen C. *The Gospel Hoax: Morton Smith's Invention of Secret Mark*. Waco, TX: Baylor University Press, 2005.

Crossan, J. D. *The Birth of Christianity: Discovering What Happened in the Years Immediately After the Execution of Jesus*. San Francisco: HarperSanFrancisco, 1999.

Davies, Stevan L. *The Gospel of Thomas: Annotated and Explained*. Woodstock, VT: SkyLight Paths, 2002.

————. *The Secret Book of John: Annotated and Explained*. Woodstock, VT: SkyLight Paths, 2005.

Dunkerley, Roderic. *Beyond the Gospels*. London: Penguin Books, 1957.

Ehrman, Bart. *Lost Christianities: The Battles for Scripture and the Faiths We Never Knew*. New York: Oxford University Press, 2003.

————. *Lost Scriptures: Books That Did Not Make It into the New Testament*. New York: Oxford University Press, 2003.

Elliott, J. K. *The Apocryphal New Testament*. Oxford: Clarendon Press, 1993.

Fitzgerald, Edward, Justin McCarthy, and Richard Le Gallienne. *The Quatrains of Omar Khayyam*. Oregon House, CA: Bardic Press, 2005.

Funk, Robert W., and Roy W. Hoover, eds. *The Five Gospels: What Did Jesus Really Say?* San Francisco: HarperSanFrancisco, 1993.

James, M. R. *The Apocryphal New Testament*. Oxford: Oxford University Press, 1955.

Khalidi, Tarif. *The Muslim Jesus: Sayings and Stories in Islamic Literature*. Cambridge, MA and London: Harvard University Press, 2001.

Koester, Helmut. *Ancient Christian Gospels: Their History and Development*. Harrisburg, PA: Trinity Press, 1990.

Layton, Bentley. *The Gnostic Scriptures: A New Translation with Annotations and Introductions*. Garden City, NY: Doubleday, 1995.

Layton, Bentley, ed. *Nag Hammadi Codex II, 2–7. Vol 1*. Leiden, NY: Brill, 1989.

Mayotte, Ricky Alan. *The Complete Jesus*. South Royalton, VT: Steerforth Press, 1997.

Meyer, Marvin. *The Gospel of Thomas: The Hidden Sayings of Jesus*. San Francisco: HarperSanFrancisco, 1992.

———. *The Unknown Sayings of Jesus*. San Francisco: HarperSanFrancisco, 1998.

Meyer, Marvin, and Richard Smith, eds. *Ancient Christian Magic*. San Francisco: HarperSanFrancisco, 1994.

Miller, Robert J., ed. *The Complete Gospels*. Sonoma, CA: Polebridge Press, 1992.

Morrice, William G. *The Hidden Sayings of Jesus*. Peabody, MA: Hendrickson, 1997.

Nadich, Judah. *Jewish Legends of the Second Commonwealth*. Philadelphia, PA: The Jewish Publication Society of America, 1983.

———. *The Legends of the Rabbis Volume 2: The First Generation after the Destruction of the Temple and Jerusalem*. Northdale, NJ: Jason Aronson, Inc., 1994.

Nurbakhsh, Javad. *Jesus in the Eyes of the Sufis*. London: Khaniqahi-Nimatullahi, 1992.

Price, Robert M. *Deconstructing Jesus*. Amherst, NY: Prometheus, 2000.

Robinson, James, ed. *The Nag Hammadi Library in English,* rev. ed. San Francisco: Harper & Row, 1988.

Robson, James. *Christ in Islam*. Oregon House, CA: Bardic Press, 2005.

Scheemelcher, Wilhelm, ed., and R. M. Wilson, trans. *New Testament Apocrypha Volume One: Gospels and Revised Writings,* rev. ed. Louisville, KY: Westminster/John Knox Press, 1991.

Smith, Andrew Phillip. *The Gospel of Philip: Annotated & Explained*. Woodstock, VT: SkyLight Paths, 2005.

———. *The Gospel of Thomas: A New Version Based on Its Inner Meaning*. Oregon House, CA: Ulysses Books, 2002.

Stroker, William D. *Extracanonical Sayings of Jesus*. Atlanta, GA: Scholars Press, 1989.

Vermes, Geza. *Jesus the Jew: A Historian's Reading of the Gospels*. London: Collins, 1973.

———. *The Religion of Jesus the Jew*. Minneapolis, MN: Fortress Press, 1993.

Wilson, Ian. *Are These the Words of Jesus?* Oxford: Lennard Publishing, 1990.

Global Spiritual Perspectives

Spiritual Perspectives on America's Role as Superpower
by the Editors at SkyLight Paths

Are we the world's good neighbor or a global bully? From a spiritual perspective, what are America's responsibilities as the only remaining superpower? Contributors:

Dr. Beatrice Bruteau • Rev. Dr. Joan Brown Campbell • Tony Campolo • Rev. Forrest Church • Lama Surya Das • Matthew Fox • Kabir Helminski • Thich Nhat Hanh • Eboo Patel • Abbot M. Basil Pennington, ocso • Dennis Prager • Rosemary Radford Ruether • Wayne Teasdale • Rev. William McD. Tully • Rabbi Arthur Waskow • John Wilson

5½ x 8½, 256 pp, Quality PB, ISBN 1-893361-81-0 **$16.95**

Spiritual Perspectives on Globalization, 2nd Edition
Making Sense of Economic and Cultural Upheaval
by Ira Rifkin; Foreword by Dr. David Little, Harvard Divinity School

What is globalization? Surveys the religious landscape, explaining in clear and non-judgmental language the beliefs that motivate spiritual leaders, activists, theologians, academics, and others involved on all sides of the issue. Includes a new Afterword and Discussion Guide designed for group use.

5½ x 8½, 256 pp, Quality PB, ISBN 1-59473-045-8 **$16.99**

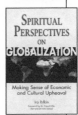

Hinduism / Vedanta

Meditation & Its Practices: A Definitive Guide to Techniques and Traditions of Meditation in Yoga and Vedanta
by Swami Adiswarananda

The complete sourcebook for exploring Hinduism's two most time-honored traditions of meditation.

6 x 9, 504 pp, HC, ISBN 1-893361-83-7 **$34.95**

The Spiritual Quest and the Way of Yoga: The Goal, the Journey and the Milestones   *by Swami Adiswarananda*

The Yoga way to attain the goal of life and overcome obstacles on the spiritual path.

6 x 9, 288 pp, HC, ISBN 1-59473-113-6 **$29.99**

Sri Ramakrishna, the Face of Silence
by Swami Nikhilananda and Dhan Gopal Mukerji
Edited with an Introduction by Swami Adiswarananda; Foreword by Dhan Gopal Mukerji II

Classic biographies present the life of Sri Ramakrishna and explain systems of Indian thought intimately connected with his life.

6 x 9, 352 pp, HC, ISBN 1-59473-115-2 **$29.99**

Sri Sarada Devi, The Holy Mother: Her Teachings and Conversations
Translated and with Notes by Swami Nikhilananda
Edited and with an Introduction by Swami Adiswarananda

Brings to life the Holy Mother's teachings on human affliction, self-control and peace.

6 x 9, 288 pp, HC, ISBN 1-59473-070-9 **$29.99**

The Vedanta Way to Peace and Happiness
by Swami Adiswarananda

Introduces the timeless teachings of Vedanta—divinity of the individual soul, unity of all existence, and oneness with the Divine.

6 x 9, 240 pp, HC, ISBN 1-59473-034-2 **$29.99**

Or phone, fax, mail or e-mail to: SKYLIGHT PATHS Publishing
Sunset Farm Offices, Route 4 • P.O. Box 237 • Woodstock, Vermont 05091
Tel: (802) 457-4000 • Fax: (802) 457-4004 • www.skylightpaths.com
Credit card orders: (800) 962-4544 (8:30AM–5:30PM ET Monday–Friday)
Generous discounts on quantity orders. SATISFACTION GUARANTEED. Prices subject to change.

Sacred Texts—SkyLight Illuminations Series

Andrew Harvey, series editor

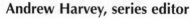

Offers today's spiritual seeker an enjoyable entry into the great classic texts of the world's spiritual traditions. Each classic is presented in an accessible translation, with facing pages of guided commentary from experts, giving you the keys you need to understand the history, context and meaning of the text. This series enables readers of all backgrounds to experience and understand classic spiritual texts directly, and to make them a part of their lives.

Bhagavad Gita: Annotated & Explained
Translation by Shri Purohit Swami; Annotation by Kendra Crossen Burroughs
Foreword by Andrew Harvey
"The very best Gita for first-time readers." —Ken Wilber. Millions of people turn daily to India's most beloved holy book, whose universal appeal has made it popular with non-Hindus and Hindus alike. This edition introduces you to the characters, explains references and philosophical terms, shares the interpretations of famous spiritual leaders and scholars, and more.
5½ x 8½, 192 pp, Quality PB, ISBN 1-893361-28-4 **$16.95**

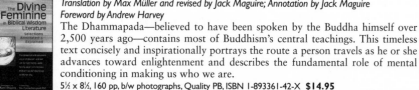

Dhammapada: Annotated & Explained
Translation by Max Müller and revised by Jack Maguire; Annotation by Jack Maguire
Foreword by Andrew Harvey
The Dhammapada—believed to have been spoken by the Buddha himself over 2,500 years ago—contains most of Buddhism's central teachings. This timeless text concisely and inspirationally portrays the route a person travels as he or she advances toward enlightenment and describes the fundamental role of mental conditioning in making us who we are.
5½ x 8½, 160 pp, b/w photographs, Quality PB, ISBN 1-893361-42-X **$14.95**

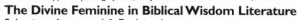

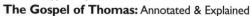

The Divine Feminine in Biblical Wisdom Literature
Selections Annotated & Explained
Translation and annotation by Rabbi Rami Shapiro; Foreword by Rev. Dr. Cynthia Bourgeault
Uses the Hebrew books of Psalms, Proverbs, Song of Songs, Ecclesiastes and Job, and the Wisdom literature books of Sirach and the Wisdom of Solomon to clarify who Wisdom is, what She teaches, and how Her words can help us live justly, wisely and with compassion.
5½ x 8½, 240 pp, Quality PB, ISBN 1-59473-109-8 **$16.99**

The Gospel of Thomas: Annotated & Explained
Translation and annotation by Stevan Davies; Foreword by Andrew Harvey
Discovered in 1945, this collection of aphoristic sayings sheds new light on the origins of Christianity and the intriguing figure of Jesus, portraying the Kingdom of God as a present fact about the world, rather than a future promise or future threat.
5½ x 8½, 192 pp, Quality PB, ISBN 1-893361-45-4 **$16.95**

Hasidic Tales: Annotated & Explained
Translation and annotation by Rabbi Rami Shapiro; Foreword by Andrew Harvey
Introduces the legendary tales of the impassioned Hasidic rabbis, which demonstrate the spiritual power of unabashed joy, offer lessons for leading a holy life, and remind us that the Divine can be found in the everyday.
5½ x 8½, 240 pp, Quality PB, ISBN 1-893361-86-1 **$16.95**

The Hebrew Prophets: Selections Annotated & Explained
Translation and annotation by Rabbi Rami Shapiro; Foreword by Zalman M. Schachter-Shalomi
Focuses on the central themes covered by all the Hebrew prophets: moving from ignorance to wisdom, injustice to justice, cruelty to compassion, and despair to joy, and challenges us to engage in justice, kindness and humility in every aspect of our lives.
5½ x 8½, 224 pp, Quality PB, ISBN 1-59473-037-7 **$16.99**

Sacred Texts—SkyLight Illuminations Series
Andrew Harvey, series editor

The Hidden Gospel of Matthew: Annotated & Explained
Translation and annotation by Ron Miller

Takes you deep into the text cherished around the world to discover the words and events that have the strongest connection to the historical Jesus. Reveals the underlying story of Matthew, a story that transcends the traditional theme of an atoning death and focuses instead on Jesus's radical call for personal transformation and social change.

5½ x 8½, 272 pp, Quality PB, ISBN 1-59473-038-5 **$16.99**

The Secret Book of John
The Gnostic Gospel—Annotated & Explained
Translation and annotation by Stevan Davies

Introduces the most significant and influential text of the ancient Gnostic religion. This central myth of Gnosticism tells the story of how God fell from perfect Oneness to imprisonment in the material world, and how by knowing our divine nature and our divine origins—that we are one with God—we reverse God's descent and find our salvation.

5½ x 8½, 208 pp, Quality PB, ISBN 1-59473-082-2 **$16.99**

Rumi and Islam: Selections from His Stories, Poems, and Discourses—Annotated & Explained
Translation and annotation by Ibrahim Gamard

Offers a new way of thinking about Rumi's poetry. Focuses on Rumi's place within the Sufi tradition of Islam, providing insight into the mystical side of the religion—one that has love of God at its core and sublime wisdom teachings as its pathways.

5½ x 8½, 240 pp, Quality PB, ISBN 1-59473-002-4 **$15.99**

Selections from the Gospel of Sri Ramakrishna
Annotated & Explained
Translation by Swami Nikhilananda; Annotation by Kendra Crossen Burroughs
Foreword by Andrew Harvey

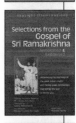

The words of India's greatest example of God-consciousness and mystical ecstasy in recent history. Introduces the fascinating world of the Indian mystic and the universal appeal of his message that has inspired millions of devotees for more than a century.

5½ x 8½, 240 pp, b/w photographs, Quality PB, ISBN 1-893361-46-2 **$16.95**

Spiritual Writings on Mary: Annotated & Explained
Annotation by Mary Ford-Grabowsky

Selections from influential writers, thinkers, and theologians—ancient and modern, from Western and Eastern backgrounds—examine the role of Mary, the mother of Jesus, as a source of inspiration in history and in life today.

5½ x 8½, 288 pp, Quality PB, ISBN 1-59473-001-6 **$16.99**

The Way of a Pilgrim: Annotated & Explained
Translation and annotation by Gleb Pokrovsky; Foreword by Andrew Harvey

This classic of Russian spirituality is the delightful account of one man who sets out to learn the prayer of the heart—also known as the "Jesus prayer"—and how the practice transforms his life.

5½ x 8½, 160 pp, Illus., Quality PB, ISBN 1-893361-31-4 **$14.95**

Zohar: Annotated & Explained
Translation and annotation by Daniel C. Matt; Foreword by Andrew Harvey

The best-selling author of *The Essential Kabbalah* brings together in one place the most important teachings of the Zohar, the canonical text of Jewish mystical tradition. Guides you step by step through the midrash, mystical fantasy, and Hebrew scripture that make up the Zohar, explaining the inner meanings in facing-page commentary.

5½ x 8½, 176 pp, Quality PB, ISBN 1-893361-51-9 **$15.99**

Midrash Fiction

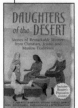

Daughters of the Desert: Tales of Remarkable Women from Christian, Jewish, and Muslim Traditions   *by Claire Rudolf Murphy, Meghan Nuttall Sayres, Mary Cronk Farrell, Sarah Conover, and Betsy Wharton*
Breathes new life into the old tales of our female ancestors in faith. Uses traditional scriptural passages as starting points, then with vivid detail fills in historical context and place. Chapters reveal the voices of Sarah, Hagar, Huldah, Esther, Salome, Mary Magdalene, Lydia, Khadija, Fatima and many more. Historical fiction ideal for readers of all ages. Quality paperback includes reader's discussion guide.
5½ x 8½, 208 pp, Quality PB, ISBN 1-59473-106-3 **$14.99**; HC, 192 pp, ISBN 1-893361-72-1 **$19.95**

The Triumph of Eve & Other Subversive Bible Tales
by Matt Biers-Ariel
Many people were taught and remember only a one-dimensional Bible. These engaging retellings are the antidote to this—they're witty, often hilarious, always profound, and invite you to grapple with questions and issues that are often hidden in the original text.
5½ x 8½, 192 pp, HC, ISBN 1-59473-040-7 **$19.99**

Also available:
The Triumph of Eve & Other Subversive Bible Tales Teacher's Guide
8½ x 11, 44 pp, PB, ISBN 1-59473-152-7 **$8.99**

Religious Etiquette / Reference

How to Be a Perfect Stranger, 3rd Edition: The Essential Religious Etiquette Handbook   *Edited by Stuart M. Matlins and Arthur J. Magida*
The indispensable guidebook to help the well-meaning guest when visiting other people's religious ceremonies. A straightforward guide to the rituals and celebrations of the major religions and denominations in the United States and Canada from the perspective of an interested guest of any other faith, based on information obtained from authorities of each religion. Belongs in every living room, library and office. Covers:
African American Methodist Churches • Assemblies of God • Bahá'í • Baptist • Buddhist • Christian Church (Disciples of Christ) • Christian Science (Church of Christ, Scientist) • Churches of Christ • Episcopalian and Anglican • Hindu • Islam • Jehovah's Witnesses • Jewish • Lutheran • Mennonite/Amish • Methodist • Mormon (Church of Jesus Christ of Latter-day Saints) • Native American/First Nations • Orthodox Churches • Pentecostal Church of God • Presbyterian • Quaker (Religious Society of Friends) • Reformed Church in America/Canada • Roman Catholic • Seventh-day Adventist • Sikh • Unitarian Universalist • United Church of Canada • United Church of Christ
6 x 9, 432 pp, Quality PB, ISBN 1-893361-67-5 **$19.95**

The Perfect Stranger's Guide to Funerals and Grieving Practices: A Guide to Etiquette in Other People's Religious Ceremonies   *Edited by Stuart M. Matlins*
6 x 9, 240 pp, Quality PB, ISBN 1-893361-20-9 **$16.95**

The Perfect Stranger's Guide to Wedding Ceremonies: A Guide to Etiquette in Other People's Religious Ceremonies   *Edited by Stuart M. Matlins*
6 x 9, 208 pp, Quality PB, ISBN 1-893361-19-5 **$16.95**

Spiritual Biography—SkyLight Lives

SkyLight Lives reintroduces the lives and works of key spiritual figures of our time—people who by their teaching or example have challenged our assumptions about spirituality and have caused us to look at it in new ways.

 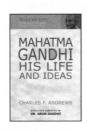  

The Life of Evelyn Underhill
An Intimate Portrait of the Groundbreaking Author of *Mysticism*
by Margaret Cropper; Foreword by Dana Greene
Evelyn Underhill was a passionate writer and teacher who wrote elegantly on mysticism, worship, and devotional life. This is the story of how she made her way toward spiritual maturity, from her early days of agnosticism to the years when her influence was felt throughout the world.
6 x 9, 288 pp, 5 b/w photos, Quality PB, ISBN 1-893361-70-5 **$18.95**

Mahatma Gandhi: His Life and Ideas
by Charles F. Andrews; Foreword by Dr. Arun Gandhi
Examines from a contemporary Christian activist's point of view the religious ideas and political dynamics that influenced the birth of the peaceful resistance movement, the primary tool that Gandhi and the people of his homeland would use to gain India its freedom from British rule.
6 x 9, 336 pp, 5 b/w photos, Quality PB, ISBN 1-893361-89-6 **$18.95**

Simone Weil: A Modern Pilgrimage
by Robert Coles
The extraordinary life of the spiritual philosopher who's been called both saint and madwoman. Robert Coles' intriguing study of Weil is an insightful portrait of the beloved and controversial thinker whose life and writings influenced many (from T. S. Eliot to Adrienne Rich to Albert Camus), and continue to inspire seekers everywhere.
6 x 9, 208 pp, Quality PB, ISBN 1-893361-34-9 **$16.95**

Zen Effects: The Life of Alan Watts
by Monica Furlong
Through his widely popular books and lectures, Alan Watts (1915–1973) did more to introduce Eastern philosophy and religion to Western minds than any figure before or since. Here is the first and only full-length biography of one of the most charismatic spiritual leaders of the twentieth century.
6 x 9, 264 pp, Quality PB, ISBN 1-893361-32-2 **$16.95**

More Spiritual Biography

Bede Griffiths: An Introduction to His Interspiritual Thought
by Wayne Teasdale 6 x 9, 288 pp, Quality PB, ISBN 1-893361-77-2 **$18.95**

Inspired Lives: Exploring the Role of Faith and Spirituality in the Lives of Extraordinary People
by Joanna Laufer and Kenneth S. Lewis 6 x 9, 256 pp, Quality PB, ISBN 1-893361-33-0 **$16.95**

Spiritual Innovators: Seventy-Five Extraordinary People Who Changed the World in
the Past Century *Edited by Ira Rifkin and the Editors at SkyLight Paths; Foreword by Robert Coles*
6 x 9, 304 pp, Quality PB, ISBN 1-893361-50-0 **$16.95**; HC, ISBN 1-893361-43-8 **$24.95**

White Fire: A Portrait of Women Spiritual Leaders in America
by Rabbi Malka Drucker; Photographs by Gay Block
7 x 10, 320 pp, 30+ b/w photos, HC, ISBN 1-893361-64-0 **$24.95**

Spirituality

Autumn: A Spiritual Biography of the Season
Edited by Gary Schmidt and Susan M. Felch; Illustrations by Mary Azarian
Rejoice in autumn as a time of preparation and reflection. Includes Wendell Berry, David James Duncan, Robert Frost, A. Bartlett Giamatti, Kimiko Hahn, P. D. James, Julian of Norwich, Garret Keizer, Tracy Kidder, Anne Lamott, May Sarton.
6 x 9, 320 pp, 5 b/w illus., Quality PB, ISBN 1-59473-118-7 **$18.99**; HC, ISBN 1-59473-005-9 **$22.99**

Awakening the Spirit, Inspiring the Soul
30 Stories of Interspiritual Discovery in the Community of Faiths
Edited by Brother Wayne Teasdale and Martha Howard, MD; Foreword by Joan Borysenko, PhD
Thirty original spiritual mini-biographies that showcase the varied ways that people come to faith—and what that means—in today's multi-religious world.
6 x 9, 224 pp, HC, ISBN 1-59473-039-3 **$21.99**

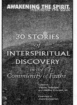

Summer: A Spiritual Biography of the Season
Edited by Gary Schmidt and Susan M. Felch; Illustrations by Mary Azarian
"A sumptuous banquet…. These selections lift up an exquisite wholeness found within an everyday sophistication."— ★ *Publishers Weekly* starred review
Includes Anne Lamott, Luci Shaw, Ray Bradbury, Richard Selzer, Thomas Lynch, Walt Whitman, Carl Sandburg, Sherman Alexie, Madeleine L'Engle, Jamaica Kincaid.
6 x 9, 304 pp, 5 b/w illus., Hardcover, ISBN 1-59473-083-0 **$21.99**

Winter: A Spiritual Biography of the Season
Edited by Gary Schmidt and Susan M. Felch; Illustrations by Barry Moser
"This outstanding anthology features top-flight nature and spirituality writers on the fierce, inexorable season of winter…. Remarkably lively and warm, despite the icy subject." — ★ *Publishers Weekly* starred review.
Includes Will Campbell, Rachel Carson, Annie Dillard, Donald Hall, Ron Hansen, Jane Kenyon, Jamaica Kincaid, Barry Lopez, Kathleen Norris, John Updike, E. B. White.
6 x 9, 288 pp, 6 b/w illus., Deluxe PB w/flaps, ISBN 1-893361-92-6 **$18.95**; HC, ISBN 1-893361-53-5 **$21.95**

The Alphabet of Paradise: An A–Z of Spirituality for Everyday Life
by Howard Cooper 5 x 7¾, 224 pp, Quality PB, ISBN 1-893361-80-2 **$16.95**

Creating a Spiritual Retirement: A Guide to the Unseen Possibilities in Our Lives
by Molly Srode 6 x 9, 208 pp, b/w photos, Quality PB, ISBN 1-59473-050-42 **$14.99**; HC, ISBN 1-893361-75-6 **$19.95**

The Geography of Faith: Underground Conversations on Religious, Political and Social Change *by Daniel Berrigan and Robert Coles; Updated introduction and afterword by the authors* 6 x 9, 224 pp, Quality PB, ISBN 1-893361-40-3 **$16.95**

God Lives in Glass: Reflections of God for Adults through the Eyes of Children
by Robert J. Landy, PhD; Foreword by Sandy Eisenberg Sasso
7 x 6, 64 pp, HC, Full-color illus., ISBN 1-893361-30-6 **$12.95**

God Within: Our Spiritual Future—As Told by Today's New Adults *Edited by Jon M. Sweeney and the Editors at SkyLight Paths* 6 x 9, 176 pp, Quality PB, ISBN 1-893361-15-2 **$14.95**

Jewish Spirituality: A Brief Introduction for Christians *by Lawrence Kushner*
5½ x 8½, 112 pp, Quality PB, ISBN 1-58023-150-0 **$12.95** *(a Jewish Lights book)*

A Jewish Understanding of the New Testament
by Rabbi Samuel Sandmel; New preface by Rabbi David Sandmel
5½ x 8½, 384 pp, Quality PB, ISBN 1-59473-048-2 **$19.99**

Journeys of Simplicity: Traveling Light with Thomas Merton, Bashō, Edward Abbey, Annie Dillard & Others *by Philip Harnden* 5 x 7¼, 128 pp, HC, ISBN 1-893361-76-4 **$16.95**

Keeping Spiritual Balance As We Grow Older: More than 65 Creative Ways to Use Purpose, Prayer, and the Power of Spirit to Build a Meaningful Retirement
by Molly and Bernie Srode 8 x 8, 224 pp, Quality PB, ISBN 1-59473-042-3 **$16.99**

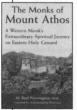

The Monks of Mount Athos: A Western Monk's Extraordinary Spiritual Journey on Eastern Holy Ground *by M. Basil Pennington, ocso; Foreword by Archimandrite Dionysios*
6 x 9, 256 pp, 10+ b/w line drawings, Quality PB, ISBN 1-893361-78-0 **$18.95**

One God Clapping: The Spiritual Path of a Zen Rabbi *by Alan Lew with Sherrill Jaffe*
5½ x 8½, 336 pp, Quality PB, ISBN 1-58023-115-2 **$16.95** *(a Jewish Lights book)*

Spirituality

Prayer for People Who Think Too Much
A Guide to Everyday, Anywhere Prayer from the World's Faith Traditions   *by Mitch Finley*
5½ x 8½, 224 pp, Quality PB, ISBN 1-893361-21-7   **$16.99**; HC, ISBN 1-893361-00-4   **$21.95**

The Shaman's Quest: Journeys in an Ancient Spiritual Practice
by Nevill Drury; with a Basic Introduction to Shamanism by Tom Cowan
5½ x 8½, 208 pp, Quality PB, ISBN 1-893361-68-3   **$16.95**

Show Me Your Way: The Complete Guide to Exploring Interfaith Spiritual Direction
by Howard A. Addison   5½ x 8½, 240 pp, Quality PB, ISBN 1-893361-41-1   **$16.95**;
HC, ISBN 1-893361-12-8   **$21.95**

Spirituality 101: The Indispensable Guide to Keeping—or Finding—Your Spiritual Life
on Campus   *by Harriet L. Schwartz, with contributions from college students at nearly thirty campuses across the United States*   6 x 9, 272 pp, Quality PB, ISBN 1-59473-000-8   **$16.99**

Spiritually Incorrect: Finding God in All the Wrong Places
by Dan Wakefield; Illus. by Marian DelVecchio
5½ x 8½, 192 pp, b/w illus., Quality PB, ISBN 1-59473-137-3   **$15.99**; HC, ISBN 1-893361-88-8   **$21.95**

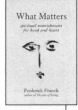

Spiritual Manifestos: Visions for Renewed Religious Life in America from Young
Spiritual Leaders of Many Faiths   *Edited by Niles Elliot Goldstein; Preface by Martin E. Marty*
6 x 9, 256 pp, HC, ISBN 1-893361-09-8   **$21.95**

A Walk with Four Spiritual Guides: Krishna, Buddha, Jesus, and Ramakrishna
by Andrew Harvey   5½ x 8½, 192 pp, 10 b/w photos & illus., Quality PB, ISBN 1-59473-138-1   **$15.99**;
HC, ISBN 1-893361-73-X   **$21.95**

What Matters: Spiritual Nourishment for Head and Heart
by Frederick Franck   5 x 7¼, 144 pp, 50+ b/w illus., HC, ISBN 1-59473-013-X   **$16.99**

Who Is My God?, 2nd Edition
An Innovative Guide to Finding Your Spiritual Identity
Created by the Editors at SkyLight Paths   6 x 9, 160 pp, Quality PB, ISBN 1-59473-014-8   **$15.99**

Spirituality—A Week Inside

Come and Sit: A Week Inside Meditation Centers
by Marcia Z. Nelson; Foreword by Wayne Teasdale
The insider's guide to meditation in a variety of different spiritual traditions. Traveling through Buddhist, Hindu, Christian, Jewish, and Sufi traditions, this essential guide takes you to different meditation centers to meet the teachers and students and learn about the practices, demystifying the meditation experience.
6 x 9, 224 pp, b/w photographs, Quality PB, ISBN 1-893361-35-7   **$16.95**

Lighting the Lamp of Wisdom: A Week Inside a Yoga Ashram
by John Ittner; Foreword by Dr. David Frawley
This insider's guide to Hindu spiritual life takes you into a typical week of retreat inside a yoga ashram to demystify the experience and show you what to expect from your own visit. Includes a discussion of worship services, meditation and yoga classes, chanting and music, work practice and more.   6 x 9, 192 pp, b/w photographs, Quality PB, ISBN 1-893361-52-7   **$15.95**; HC, ISBN 1-893361-37-3   **$24.95**

Making a Heart for God: A Week Inside a Catholic Monastery
by Dianne Aprile; Foreword by Brother Patrick Hart, ocso
This essential guide to experiencing life in a Catholic monastery takes you to the Abbey of Gethsemani—the Trappist monastery in Kentucky that was home to author Thomas Merton—to explore the details. "More balanced and informative than the popular *The Cloister Walk* by Kathleen Norris."
—*Choice: Current Reviews for Academic Libraries*
6 x 9, 224 pp, b/w photographs, Quality PB, ISBN 1-893361-49-7   **$16.95**; HC, ISBN 1-893361-14-4   **$21.95**

Waking Up: A Week Inside a Zen Monastery
by Jack Maguire; Foreword by John Daido Loori, Roshi
An essential guide to what it's like to spend a week inside a Zen Buddhist monastery.
6 x 9, 224 pp, b/w photographs, Quality PB, ISBN 1-893361-55-1   **$16.95**;
HC, ISBN 1-893361-13-6   **$21.95**

Spiritual Practice

Divining the Body
Reclaim the Holiness of Your Physical Self *by Jan Phillips*
A practical and inspiring guidebook for connecting the body and soul in spiritual practice. Leads you into a milieu of reverence, mystery and delight, helping you discover a redeemed sense of self.
8 x 8, 256 pp, Quality PB, ISBN 1-59473-080-6 **$16.99**

Finding Time for the Timeless
Spirituality in the Workweek *by John McQuiston II*

Simple, refreshing stories that provide you with examples of how you can refocus and enrich your daily life using prayer or meditation, ritual and other forms of spiritual practice. 5½ x 6½, 208 pp, HC, ISBN 1-59473-035-0 **$17.99**

The Gospel of Thomas: A Guidebook for Spiritual Practice
by Ron Miller; Translations by Stevan Davies
An innovative guide to bring a new spiritual classic into daily life. Offers a way to translate the wisdom of the Gospel of Thomas into daily practice, manifesting in your life the same consciousness revealed in Jesus of Nazareth. Written for readers of all religious backgrounds, this guidebook will help you to apply Jesus's wisdom to your own life and to the world around you.
6 x 9, 160 pp, Quality PB, ISBN 1-59473-047-4 **$14.99**

The Knitting Way: A Guide to Spiritual Self-Discovery
by Linda Skolnik and Janice MacDaniels
Through sharing stories, hands-on explorations and daily cultivation, Skolnik and MacDaniels help you see beyond the surface of a simple craft in order to discover ways in which nuances of knitting can apply to the larger scheme of life and spirituality. Includes original knitting patterns.
7 x 9, 240 pp, Quality PB, ISBN 1-59473-079-2 **$16.99**

Earth, Water, Fire, and Air: Essential Ways of Connecting to Spirit
by Cait Johnson 6 x 9, 224 pp, HC, ISBN 1-893361-65-9 **$19.95**

Forty Days to Begin a Spiritual Life
Today's Most Inspiring Teachers Help You on Your Way
Edited by Maura Shaw and the Editors at SkyLight Paths; Foreword by Dan Wakefield
7 x 9, 144 pp, Quality PB, ISBN 1-893361-48-9 **$16.95**

Labyrinths from the Outside In
Walking to Spiritual Insight—A Beginner's Guide
by Donna Schaper and Carole Ann Camp
6 x 9, 208 pp, b/w illus. and photographs, Quality PB, ISBN 1-893361-18-7 **$16.95**

Practicing the Sacred Art of Listening: A Guide to Enrich Your Relationships and Kindle Your Spiritual Life—The Listening Center Workshop
by Kay Lindahl 8 x 8, 176 pp, Quality PB, ISBN 1-893361-85-3 **$16.95**

The Sacred Art of Bowing: Preparing to Practice
by Andi Young 5½ x 8½, 128 pp, b/w illus., Quality PB, ISBN 1-893361-82-9 **$14.95**

The Sacred Art of Chant: Preparing to Practice
by Ana Hernandez 5½ x 8½, 192 pp, Quality PB, ISBN 1-59473-036-9 **$15.99**

The Sacred Art of Fasting: Preparing to Practice
by Thomas Ryan, CSP 5½ x 8½, 192 pp, Quality PB, ISBN 1-59473-078-4 **$15.99**

The Sacred Art of Listening: Forty Reflections for Cultivating a Spiritual Practice
by Kay Lindahl; Illustrations by Amy Schnapper
8 x 8, 160 pp, Illus., Quality PB, ISBN 1-893361-44-6 **$16.99**

Sacred Speech: A Practical Guide for Keeping Spirit in Your Speech
by Rev. Donna Schaper 6 x 9, 176 pp, Quality PB, ISBN 1-59473-068-7 **$15.99**;
HC, ISBN 1-893361-74-8 **$21.95**

Spiritual Poetry—The Mystic Poets

Experience these mystic poets as you never have before. Each beautiful, compact book includes: A brief introduction to the poet's time and place; a summary of the major themes of the poet's mysticism and religious tradition; essential selections from the poet's most important works; and an appreciative preface by a contemporary spiritual writer.

   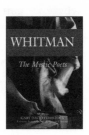

Hafiz: The Mystic Poets
Preface by Ibrahim Gamard
Hafiz is known throughout the world as Persia's greatest poet, with sales of his poems in Iran today only surpassed by those of the Qur'an itself. His probing and joyful verse speaks to people from all backgrounds who long to taste and feel divine love and experience harmony with all living things.
5 x 7¼, 144 pp, HC, ISBN 1-59473-009-1 **$16.99**

Hopkins: The Mystic Poets
Preface by Rev. Thomas Ryan, CSP
Gerard Manley Hopkins, Christian mystical poet, is beloved for his use of fresh language and startling metaphors to describe the world around him. Although his verse is lovely, beneath the surface lies a searching soul, wrestling with and yearning for God.
5 x 7¼, 112 pp, HC, ISBN 1-59473-010-5 **$16.99**

Tagore: The Mystic Poets
Preface by Swami Adiswarananda
Rabindranath Tagore is often considered the "Shakespeare" of modern India. A great mystic, Tagore was the teacher of W. B. Yeats and Robert Frost, the close friend of Albert Einstein and Mahatma Gandhi, and the winner of the Nobel Prize for Literature. This beautiful sampling of Tagore's two most important works, *The Gardener* and *Gitanjali,* offers a glimpse into his spiritual vision that has inspired people around the world.
5 x 7¼, 144 pp, HC, ISBN 1-59473-008-3 **$16.99**

Whitman: The Mystic Poets
Preface by Gary David Comstock
Walt Whitman was the most innovative and influential poet of the nineteenth century. This beautiful sampling of Whitman's most important poetry from *Leaves of Grass,* and selections from his prose writings, offers a glimpse into the spiritual side of his most radical themes—love for country, love for others, and love of Self.
5 x 7¼, 192 pp, HC, ISBN 1-59473-041-5 **$16.99**

About SKYLIGHT PATHS Publishing

SkyLight Paths Publishing is creating a place where people of different spiritual traditions come together for challenge and inspiration, a place where we can help each other understand the mystery that lies at the heart of our existence.

Through spirituality, our religious beliefs are increasingly becoming a part of our lives—rather than *apart* from our lives. While many of us may be more interested than ever in spiritual growth, we may be less firmly planted in traditional religion. Yet, we do want to deepen our relationship to the sacred, to learn from our own as well as from other faith traditions, and to practice in new ways.

SkyLight Paths sees both believers and seekers as a community that increasingly transcends traditional boundaries of religion and denomination—people wanting to learn from each other, *walking together, finding the way.*

For your information and convenience, at the back of this book we have provided a list of other SkyLight Paths books you might find interesting and useful. They cover the following subjects:

Buddhism / Zen	Gnosticism	Mysticism
Catholicism	Hinduism /	Poetry
Children's Books	Vedanta	Prayer
Christianity	Inspiration	Religious Etiquette
Comparative	Islam / Sufism	Retirement
Religion	Judaism / Kabbalah /	Spiritual Biography
Current Events	Enneagram	Spiritual Direction
Earth-Based	Meditation	Spirituality
Spirituality	Midrash Fiction	Women's Interest
Global Spiritual	Monasticism	Worship
Perspectives		

Or phone, fax, mail or e-mail to: SKYLIGHT PATHS Publishing
Sunset Farm Offices, Route 4 • P.O. Box 237 • Woodstock, Vermont 05091
Tel: (802) 457-4000 • Fax: (802) 457-4004 • www.skylightpaths.com
Credit card orders: **(800) 962-4544** (8:30AM–5:30PM ET Monday–Friday)
Generous discounts on quantity orders. SATISFACTION GUARANTEED. Prices subject to change.

For more information about each book,
visit our website at www.skylightpaths.com